Start Out Strong

The simple & easy guide to manage the money in your small business

- Avoid Costly 1st Timer Mistakes -

By Vi Nguyen

Copyright

© 2022 12Descartes Pty Ltd

ISBN: 978-1-922339-02-7

Cover design © 12Descartes Pty Ltd

Author: Vi Nguyen

Editor: E Syme

Published July 2022

Imprint: Useful Money Stuff Books

The Useful Money Stuff website address is: www.usefulmoneystuff.com

Version: 2022-07-31

Disclaimer

Table of Contents

INTRODUCTION

The Failure Rate is Real..9

Why Run a Business?..15

Problems? Nope, Not All for Me...23

START HERE

Initial Decisions...29

Structure   30

Cash or Accrual   35

Be Separate   38

How it All Works..43

Who's Who?...51

Tax Authority   51

Accountant   56

Bookkeeper   63

Lawyer   64

Bank   66

3 Steps to Set Up **69**

    Step 1 - Open an Account   70

    Step 2 - Select Accounting Software   71

    Step 3 - Start Recording   76

KEEPING A FINANCIAL DIARY

Set Up Your Financial Refrigerator **79**

    Revenue / Income   80

    Expense   80

    Asset   81

    Liability   83

    Account Creation   84

Keep Your Proof **93**

Regular Dates **99**

Enter Data **103**

    Ins and Outs   103

    Dates   106

    Account   107

    Stock / Inventory Management   108

    Quantity and Unit Price   113

    Taxation   116

Check It **125**

    Bank Reconciliation   129

You've Got Records **139**

Manage Your Business Like a Boss **141**

    Collecting Payments   144

    Bills to Pay   146

    Stock or Inventory Management   147

    Filings and Lodgments   150

PRACTICE RUN TIME

Try it Yourself **153**

    Social Media Influencer   155

    Gig Workers / Independent Contractors / Consultants   164

    Products Business   172

YOU'VE GOT... INFO

A Profitable Business **181**

The Failure Rate is Real

Being in business is hard.

Surviving in business is even harder with approximately 50% of businesses failing in their first five years.

That's a scary thought, isn't it?

To think that your dreams to create something new, to provide a valuable service or to create a customer experience may just become one of those forgotten failures is a daunting thought.

And it's not only dreams but it's the hard work. The long nights and time with friends and family sacrificed so that you can work on building your new venture and keeping it afloat.

The amount of effort that goes into building a business cannot be underestimated—whether it's running a self-service laundry, baking custom cookies, playing in gigs, selling artwork, making hotdogs or going out on your own as a consultant.

In every business, what's common is the time, invested by you, into making it a success.

But the failure rate is real and let's unpack that.

Failure in a business is very individual. A business can fail for many reasons. It could be a once-in-a-lifetime event that changes behavior, like a pandemic that may restrict people from leaving their homes to patronize the restaurants they usually do. Or it could be a slow burn, where customers turn away from you and change their mind to try out a new retailer or brand, never to come back.

And you can't ever be too big to fail.

Multi-national companies making billions in sales and those operating for over 30 years have filed for bankruptcy previously. They have people with fancy qualifications that manage them.

But, if such large companies can fail, where does that leave you?

It leaves you... with you.

It's your management that will steer your business. Some situations are tougher than others and it's about being able to weather the storm that comes with running a business. Making smart decisions will be likely to help your business survive the storm until it can sail safely.

If you're running a restaurant and the once-in-a-lifetime pandemic event hits, would you make a decision to offer take-out as some businesses did?

Similarly, if you ran a hot-dog stand and you noticed that slowly, customers were turning away in favor of healthier options, would you then start modifying your menu to include healthier options, to bring customers back?

Businesses that adapt to their environment, thanks to the good decisions of those managing them, survive. But they also have something else.

Cash, the lifeblood of a business.

Cash helps your business continue to survive - to pay its bills, even if there's a period where your business isn't making much money. And accounting - the management of not only cash but the ins and outs of your business is crucial to staying on track.

Seriously, which large corporation doesn't have a specialized accounting function? Or what business doesn't have an accountant?

Because businesses that survive and thrive know that money management is not just a mere afterthought - it is an integral part of running a business. Just like sales and marketing.

And that leads us to the first-time freelancer or small business owner's dilemma.

Failure through not managing money properly which comes from not being able to understand how money works. From who plays what roles, where you fit in, what your obligations are and what to do. Essentially, where do you start?

You start here.

The finances of your business, even when you're starting out, is one of the 'scarier' things to do because it's a minefield of jargon and perhaps, 'numbers aren't your thing'. But those who don't manage their finances properly or just avoid it altogether can quickly find themselves falling into a dark pit of despair.

A pit of despair that features some unsavory characters like bankruptcy, tax authorities demanding you respond to their letters and the people who, for some reason or another, want to just delight in your misery.

These are problems you don't need in your life, given that you're running a business and that's hard enough.

So, let's get you started on understanding your business's money. It's one step in the right direction.

This book is written to help you understand your business's money so that you can avoid this dark pit of despair and perhaps, equip yourself with knowledge about money so that when your business faces its own storms, it can survive enough just to see the sunshine that awaits.

Why Run a Business?

When people start a business, their responses vary but they're usually:

"I've always wanted to go out on my own..."

"It's been a dream to be able to open..."

"Finally, I get to change people's lives and have an impact by..."

It's true. Running a business usually is a lifelong dream for many people. Going out on your own to create something that will have an impact on someone else's life is fulfilling.

But let's not lose sight of what a business *really* is.

A business is an activity to make, buy and sell services or products. Its end goal is to **make a profit.**

This isn't some hard-nosed money-making corporate speak but a real fact that means a business can continue what it's doing so that it can survive and one day, thrive.

Profit to a business is like what water is to your body—you need it for your survival. But what is profit?

It's an interesting concept and one that's crucial to know.

Let's say you work for someone, let's call this person, YBB to represent, Your Big Boss.

YBB pays you $23 an hour. And let's say you work full-time for YBB and when payday comes this week, you get your paycheck of $697. Your full earnings were $851 but YBB took out $154 to pay to the tax office as your part payment towards your end-of-year taxes.

So many numbers! Confused already?

Let's focus on the main things and break them up.

➡ Your paycheck represents your 'earnings' for the week. This is the $851 number, not the smaller amount that is paid out to you. Your earnings are what you make from your efforts and activities in working for YBB. In a business, this would be called income, revenue or earnings.
Unfortunately, in the accounting world, there are a lot of

words that mean the same thing or a similar thing. You'll soon see that this is an annoying problem.

➡ Taxes are taken out of your earnings. I like to think of it as a requirement set by your mother to give her a slice of cake if you ever make cake! So this $154 (a slice of cake) is taken out of your earnings (the total cake).

➡ Finally, you get the amount that goes into your bank account ($697) which is your earnings with the part that contributes to your tax payment taken out.

Here are the three parts you need to know and their 'official' names:

➡ Gross Earnings/Income/Revenue—This is what you earn from your efforts in total. Without anything taken out. Kind of like the whole cake when you bake one.

➡ Taxation—This is something that's taken out and the amount that's taken out depends on a number of rules set by your tax authority. It's part of business, but it's only when you make or earn money (just like mom taking a piece of the cake if there is cake to start off with). This is the slice of cake that the tax authorities take and how big this slice is depends on a number of rules that aren't covered in this book.

➡ Net Earnings—The word 'net' just means the remainder left over. This is the cake leftover.

Awesome!

We've learnt some of the keywords that come with a business. But when you work for someone else, what you consider is generally one-sided, the part where the money comes in from the sale (of your services).

The other side is spending. Where money is spent in your business to make the money that comes in.

Confused yet?

Let's bring it back to working for YBB. Let's say YBB now wants you to be a contractor, not an employee, because they only want you to perform certain tasks.

YBB says to you that you can bill them for the time you work on your tasks directly. It seems pretty standard and you don't really see that it's much of a change. You decide to charge $23 an hour on your bill to YBB, because nothing really has changed right?

But... you work from your share house now as a contractor. You've also rented a laptop to do your work on and it costs $6 a week. You're now also spending $64 on internet a month, just so that you can do daily video conferencing calls and upload your work electronically. You also notice that your electricity bill has gone up by $5 a week after you became a contractor. Furthermore, you've rented the spare room to do your work in at $25 a week.

Phew! You didn't have to pay all of this previously because you just walked into the office which was a mile away and did your work there.

So let's think about it more. You're technically a business.

➡ You're selling your time at $23 an hour.

➡ But you're also spending money in order to sell your time. You're spending $6 a week on your laptop, $25 a week on room hire, $5 on electricity and $64 a month on internet. If we divide the monthly internet to display a weekly amount, it would be $14.73 ($64 divided by 4.345). This is a total of $50.73 a week in spending.

➡ If you continue to work 37 hours as a contractor each week, you'll still bring in $851. But you now have to consider your costs – this is spending that's done for the purpose of bringing in your income. Which leaves you with $800.21.

➡ Is this good/bad? Well... it's worse than before because your effort is really bringing in less money. When you were an employee, you brought in $851 in a week. As a contractor, you're *really* only bringing in $800.21 after you account for your costs and technically, you're earning less for the same work. This $800.21 is called profit. **Profit is what you aim for in business, it's the money left over from what you earned after you take away the costs involved.** But that's not too bad of a result, right? You get $800.21 in your pocket while previously with the employer, you only got $697 after they took away your tax.

➡ Ahhh... well, you still have to pay tax if you're a contractor or self-employed but the timing may be different and how it's calculated may differ. Let's say tax as a self-employed contractor amounts to $125.63 a week. This means that you're really looking at taking home $674.58. That's $22.42 less a week. Or $1165.84 less a year.

Running a business means making a profit and in making a profit, you need to consider the numbers and consider how much it's costing you to make your sales in the first place.

In the above situation with YBB, you've still made a profit but it doesn't seem like the 'contractor' path is financially the same as your employee path, even if you're selling it for the same hourly rate. You really should negotiate with YBB to increase your rate to cover your costs and to get the same end result as you did when you were an employee!

Calculating a profit is easier when you've got fewer costs and there's only one source of money coming in.

Things can come unstuck when you're working with a larger volume and making heaps of sales to many different people and when you've got heaps of costs coming in—that you're not tracking.

You might find that you just break-even (when you don't make any money), or you make a loss (when your income doesn't cover your costs).

Let's say you produce amateur video content that you post up on various video sharing and social media platforms. You make money primarily through the advertisements that are served on these platforms. Business has been going well for the last two years. In the first year, your videos brought in $20,000 of advertising income and they only cost in total $5000 to produce! A profit of $15,000 for last year.

The second year was a bit different. You wanted to capitalize on your previous videos' successes so you upped the budget and spent $10,000 creating a bunch of new videos to put up. Unfortunately, advertisers didn't spend that much in the second year so you only brought in $10,000 in advertising income. This isn't a profit and it isn't a loss. It's called a break-even.

A break-even is when your costs equal your income. It means that your efforts and time didn't make you any money. If you were to sit on a chair doing nothing for that year and not spend any money and not make any money - it would have been the same result as your second year as a video content creator.

Now, this year, you're a bit wiser. You haven't spent so much on video creation—only $5000. Unfortunately, with more video creators flooding the platforms, your videos aren't getting many views and you were only paid $2000 this year in advertising income. Ahh... life as a content creator is cruel isn't it?

The important thing to note is that you haven't made a profit or even broke even. You've made a loss. It means you've spent more than the money that came in.

That's a bad thing, in general, because if it continues in that way, your business is on its way out of existence.

And you don't want your business to be another failure statistic.

While you may start a business to fulfill a personal reason, you should operate and run a business to make a profit - to ensure its survival so that your dream can live on.

Problems? Nope, Not *All* for Me

Business is all about dealing with problems.

Problems like what to sell, how to improve your product or services, how to expand, how to support your customers better and the list goes on.

But, there are a certain group of problems that many first-time business owners face. Examples of these problems are:

➡ Receiving a letter from the tax office saying that you owe a certain amount in tax but you're not sure if you do and you don't have the cash to pay such a large amount in one go. And then, receiving follow-up letter after follow-up letter with final notice sent.

➡ Making heaps of sales but struggling to have cash in the bank to pay your bills on time.

➡ Receiving a lot of bills and having trouble keeping up with their due dates so you keep missing their payment deadline resulting in interest added.

➡ Receiving a penalty notice from authorities for not paying entitlements correctly and an interest charge on any shortfall.

While each of these problems requires individual attention, there's often one thing in common that stresses people out.

Not knowing the answer and not knowing how to get the answer.

To know the answer and know how to get the answer—with the first example, your accountant would need to figure out the tax owed. With the second, you'd need to understand how quickly you're collecting cash from sales on credit. With the third, you need to know the bills you have and upcoming dates and finally, with the fourth example, you need to be able to know how much you did pay and whether it was in fact a shortfall.

This all comes down to **having information**. And this information comes from your **record-keeping - the record-keeping of financial information of your business**. This is where you record the goings on in your business—the sales made, the bills received and any other inflows and outflows from doing your business activity.

Without record keeping, the information that you or your accountant needs to rely on isn't there and it then needs to be reconstructed by looking back at bank statements and other information. Which takes a long time and golly, such an activity would be very costly in terms of time and money.

What's easier?

Doing your business's record-keeping (or having a bookkeeper do it)! When record-keeping is done regularly and consistently, you store the information that can be called upon, not only for your own needs, but by your accountant and government authorities to answer those gnarly questions or if they don't answer it directly, they may form the background information that then helps someone get to the answer. In fact, in some parts, keeping records is a mandated requirement.

Unfortunately, many new business owners never do record-keeping.

It's one of those things that are too hard (where do you even start? what's the process?) or maybe too boring (typing in numbers into a table or form? I'd rather do something else!). But, if not done and problems emerge... that's when people start stressing and in some cases, it looks like they're about to explode.

When you start your business or if you've already started, put your record-keeping as a priority, an integral part of running your business.

Think of keeping financial records like keeping a diary, but with numbers. You might keep a food diary if you're monitoring what you eat and your water intake. If you're unsure as to why you're feeling a bit tired, you can reference your diary to see if you've consumed enough of the right types of foods to help bring your energy levels up.

Financial record-keeping helps you reference the important information in your business - without record-keeping, it's like wandering into a maze and not knowing where you're going but you keep going in and hope that you might get out one day. But soon, you realize that you have no idea what this maze looks like and you don't have a map, let alone the knowledge to get out. So you panic and never come back out. You're lost in the maze forever.

Dealing with problems is part of business, and having the information to deal with your problems makes it less likely that you're going to be tossing and turning at night losing sleep.

And that relieves, you, the new business owner from a lot of stress. From not knowing the answer, or not knowing how to get to the answer.

So, do your record-keeping (we'll learn how to do some basic record-keeping later in this book). It means that problems related to managing your finances are controlled, and for many, these problems are the most painful.

Initial Decisions

Before you even start record-keeping, you need to make some decisions and these are decisions that will affect how you keep records.

They're decisions that are big decisions and are similar to decisions about where to live. When you make such a decision, it affects your lifestyle. Let's say you make a decision to uproot your family and live in a remote desert, that would then mean that you might not have access to many services but you would have some solitude. Once you make such a decision, it's a pain to then change this decision and move elsewhere because you then have to pack and then transfer all your belongings.

Because these initial decisions are important decisions affecting your record-keeping that are quite troublesome to change later on, it's crucial that you make these initial decisions carefully.

As every individual situation is unique, seeking and speaking to a professional advisor may assist you in making these decisions.

Let's go through the three major initial decisions you need to make when you start a business (and before you do your record-keeping).

Structure

You might have heard the word 'business structure' a few times and it's not the easiest concept to understand.

Essentially, it's like saying that your business is being born because a stream of activities of selling and buying is occurring or going to occur, but who is responsible for these activities and how are they set up?

To understand this concept in an easier way, let's use the example of the activity of selling hot-dogs - the humble hot-dog stand.

Let's say you want to set up a hot-dog stand. You've quit your job and found a location that you can use and want to start. You register your business name with the relevant authorities and start trading as a sole trader or sole proprietor. That's a business structure which means that you, as a person, are operating a business. It's easy to start (you might need to check what you need in terms of registering names etc...) but generally, you can start straight away and the money that your 'business's makes is generally considered your 'self-employment' income. It's not considered to be generally separate from you as a person. Because you are the business.

Easy right?

Let's say you now go into partnership with your friend, BFF. BFF sees that you're quite busy and has offered to work with you as a partner. As part of the partnership, they'll bring in another hot-dog cart and you'll both be able to take advantage of bulk buying discounts since you're a bigger group now than before. This business structure is called a partnership - it's when two or more people join together to do business activities.

This involves more people and requires more paperwork, such as a partnership agreement that might state how much you share in costs and income, but again, it's relatively simple to start one and you start one by working together.

A bit more complicated but nothing too hard to understand.

Now let's move onto the 'faceless' business.

You and your BFF are doing really well and selling heaps of hot-dogs but one day, there's a new hot-dog cart a block away. You walk up to the person serving at the cart and introduce yourself.

After all, business owners have it tough and it's good to have a chat. But you realize that the person serving is an employee - they don't own the cart. So you ask the server who owns it and... they just shrug and say "Meh".

That's not an answer you're going to settle for. After a bit of research late at night, you find out that the owner of the new hot-dog cart business is "HDC123 FAKE BUSINESS LLC". The owner is who, exactly?

That's the final structure we'll look at. It's called a corporate group. It's where a real-life identifiable person doesn't own the business but instead it's an invisible entity, kind of like a ghost. But... not really.

A corporate entity is like a person - it can enter into contracts and buy and sell stuff in its name, but it's formed by legal documents that bring it into existence. If we're going to use magical metaphors, it's like casting a spell to create a ghost that can buy and sell stuff. But, the ghost belongs to a certain 'owner' or 'owners' who can benefit from any ghostly things it does.

In corporate groups, the owner or owners of the entity that is formed is usually called a shareholder or stockholder.

This just got complicated. And it doesn't stop there. A corporate structure can have variations. For example, in the US a corporate structure that may be available to be formed is a limited liability company (LLC) while another one is called a corporation. In Australia, there are private companies (usually called proprietary limited companies with the abbreviation "Pty Ltd" at the end of their name) and public companies (usually with the abbreviation "Ltd" at the end of their name).

You can't understand that your beloved hot-dog stand is competing with a ghost and so, you end up finding out that HDC123 FAKE BUSINESS LLC is actually run by your ex-friend, Frenemy.

Frenemy created a corporate group because they wanted some protection against legal claims on their asset, you see, Frenemy has a lovely 6-bedroom house that they want to protect, in case they get sued for a bad hot-dog.

Mmm... Frenemy is smart. Don't you hate that in a frenemy!

The business structure you choose impacts how complicated your record-keeping may get and the administration work involved. But, it can have certain benefits and disadvantages.

The sole trader / sole-proprietor / self-employed individual is easy to start but what happens if they sell a rotten hot-dog and someone gets sick? If they get sued, whatever they own as a person may be at risk. Remember, they are the business so they're also responsible personally when things go bad.

How about the partnership with your BFF. Well? What happens when your BFF decides that they no longer want to work with you because they've gone vegan? They'll want to pull out of the partnership and then what happens to the second cart they brought with them? They'll need to exit and we know that relationships can get messy.

And the ghost? Summoned through a spelling-binding chant by usually an attorney waving their wand of registration papers and legal jargon and poof! You have your company or corporate entity. Generally, providing its owners with protection over their property but the ghost says "AaAaAahhh" when it realizes that with it existing, it needs to fill in a whole heap of paperwork... for the rest of its existence. Can it just disappear? Nope, not without a series of forms being filled out!

Now, let's get back to you.

You have some important decisions to make about your business structure. How will your business activities be contained? With you - as a sole-proprietor, with others in a partnership, in an invisible entity of a company or corporate entity with the superpower to protect your assets, or another type of entity that's available to you in your area...

Once you get all your necessary registrations done to have your entity up and running (and this book doesn't cover the legal stuff, please consult a qualified professional), write down the business structure you have chosen here:

_____

Well done! Let's move onto the next section for another initial decision you need to make.

Cash or Accrual

When you set up an accounting system (more on that later) or even when you might have to fill out some forms relating to your business, a key decision you have to make is whether you're using the "cash method" or "accrual method" of accounting.

What? This is "A-Cruel-Accounting!" Is this some bizarre and lame accounting joke? Yes. Yes, it is.

In all seriousness, it's a key decision because it sets up how your record-keeping is done.

When you do record-keeping there are a whole bunch of decisions to be made. One of those major decisions is **when to record something as a sale or a purchase.**

If you select the 'cash method' of accounting, you're saying that you only record a sale when you have received the cash in your bank account. And likewise, you'll only record a purchase if it's gone out of your bank account and been paid.

You scratch your head. Isn't this how it works anyhow? Isn't cash the way people record stuff? Like you sell if money comes in and you spend when money comes out.

Kind of, but you've forgotten a major thing - cash flow versus the contract.

Let's say that you sell artwork and you've signed a once-in-a-lifetime contract with a hotel group for 10 works of art to be displayed on their lobby walls. You deliver the artwork as part of the contract and the contract states that they're going to pay you $20,000 once the artwork is received.

So here you are. You've signed a contract. Delivered your part under the contract and now just waiting for payment.

Have you made a sale? Even if you haven't received payment?

If you choose the "accrual method" of accounting when doing your record-keeping, then yes. You would create an invoice to send to the hotel group once the artwork was delivered and it's the date of this invoice that would be recorded as the date a sale of $20,000 was made. Not the date 60 days later.

But what happens 60-days later when your payment is due and the hotel group refuses to pay you?

In accrual accounting, you've recorded a sale but you'll have to collect the money that's owing to you. If you can't collect, then it becomes a bad debt and you've lost money. If you were using cash accounting, the sale would have never been recorded in the first place because it's only a sale if cash is received.

Can you see the difference?

One method is more conservative - the cash method, because sales or bills are only recorded when money goes in or out. But the cash method might not be as relevant or timely. When the contract was signed and the product delivered, the sale was technically made and if payment isn't received, you could start the debt collection process. With accrual accounting, you get an earlier timing of sales but one that might reflect the timing of the goings on in your business more accurately.

The cash method is more simple and straightforward while the accrual method may provide more relevant and timely insights.

Sometimes you don't get a choice to choose the cash or accrual method, usually if your business is a larger organization, but if you do, that's a decision for you (and your advisor, if any) to make.

Once you've made your decision, record it below:

_____

Well done! Let's move onto the next section now.

Be Separate

Finally, you're at the end of the three initial decisions. This final part isn't necessarily a decision, but rather it is general practice that you should do to avoid problems now and in the future.

The general practice is that you should keep your business activities separate from your personal activities and as a result, your records for business should be strictly business, not personal. I believe there's a saying for this "don't mix business with pleasure" and this saying applies in the record-keeping realm too.

The thing is that it's quite easy to fall into the trap of mixing business and personal affairs, especially if your business structure is a sole proprietorship or if you're the sole owner of a company. Here are examples of people not keeping their business affairs separate:

➡ Setting up a separate business bank account and seeing that there's quite a bit of money in there so you use a little bit here and there to pay for food, snack and little treats for yourself. This action muddies the line of separation as the funds in the business bank account belong to the business and they're not to be used for personal treats, even for the owner!

➡ Purchasing something for the business and not having a business card available so you use your personal bank card. Again, like the above, this action does muddy the line of separation because you're using your own personal funds to pay for something used in the business.

➡ Not setting up a separate bank account for the business, just because you can't be bothered, and using your personal account to receive any funds or pay for any spending for the business. This is easily done when starting out but what this does is create more work for you later on if you're going to separate out what's business and what's not. Imagine working through each line of your bank statement to decide, is this business or not? and then tallying it all up and taking hours to do so. Not something you want to do during your free time.

➡ Taking stock home to be used for personal reasons. For example, if you've bought 40 hot-dog buns and 40 hot-dogs for the business and you take 20 of each back to your place for a neighborhood party. Property of the business should belong to the business. When you take away business property for personal use, you're blurring the lines between what belongs to the business and what's yours - you're pretty much saying, through your actions, that you and the business are really just the one.

And this presents a huge, huge, problem.

If you've established your business as a company, the asset protection that generally comes with a company structure can potentially be lost if it is argued that your company isn't treated as a separate entity. When people co-mingle their business and personal assets, personal assets like your car or house can be at-risk if your business was sued.

You should also separate out your business and personal activities, even if you are a sole proprietor. You and what you own are considered 'the business's in a legal sense but in record-keeping, it's important to separate the business from the personal so you get information that represents your business solely.

And another problem that comes from mixing business and personal use is additionally unnecessary work in identifying, sorting, categorizing and calculating. It's similar to having a pile of 2,000 mixed clothing and then sorting it into two different closets. It's an all-day to all-week kinda job.

Which is easily avoidable if you separate out your activities. What does this mean?

Having a separate bank account for your business from the beginning. Any money that comes in and out of the business should be traceable to that account. Any property of the business belongs to the business. There isn't any sharing of cash or property between the owner or the business in a 'casual' kind of way.

If you're unsure whether you're keeping things separate, one of the tests you should do is this:

Imagine that your business is a separate person - a friend. But this friend isn't like your typical best friend. This friend likes to keep to themselves - they don't like sharing. But you want to keep this person as your friend but also respect their wishes. If your business is this person, would you be comfortable taking 20 of their hot-dog buns and 20 of their hot-dogs home to cater for a party?

Absolutely not.

The friendship would end. And there's your test - if the friendship ends, you haven't kept your affairs separate from your business and you are welcoming in the potential for wasted time and effort and potentially risking your own personal assets from protection.

This is not something that you want to be dealing with, especially if it can be easily avoided.

So remember, make sure that business activities have their own space and that your personal activities do not interfere.

How it All Works

One of the hardest things to do when starting a new business is to figure out how it all works and where you fit in. Especially when it comes to finance and money matters.

So... here's how it all works.

Let's start at the most basic level and we'll use a social media content creator or influencer as an example of a business (and yes, contrary to what people think – it is a business).

This social media influencing business is run by Star. And they've already made their three decisions, they're going to:

· Operate as a sole proprietor, let's keep it simple!

· Do cash accounting, why make it harder right?

· Keep things separate. It's just easier!

Star starts out posting a few funny videos online and their videos get a few views and over a month, they've got a sizable number of followers commenting actively on their videos and posts.

In the beginning, Star used their phone to create posts but they purchase new equipment 💰 🖥️ to make better content.

They also start reaching out to companies to do collaborations and to advertise their products to their followers. In the following month, Star makes a deal with five companies to collaborate with. As part of the collaboration, the companies will each pay Star $1000 💰 to post twice to Star's followers within a 6-month period. The money will be transferred by each company once the second post is completed.

This is the first time that Star has 'made a deal' so they decide to put it in writing, just in case things go badly. Star hires the services of a lawyer 💰 🖥️ to write up a standard contract and these contracts 🖥️ are sent to the companies.

Star continues to create content 💰 🖥️ and sell advertising and marketing services 💰 🖥️ over the next few years.

In business, like Star, you'll be doing activities and these activities will have a financial impact. The activities that do have a financial impact have been shown with the money bag emoji above.

In purchasing equipment, Star is spending money. In collaborating, Star is selling advertising space to the companies and is making money. When Star hires the lawyer, they're spending money.

These are all activities that have happened.

But in a few years' time, let alone by the end of the night, how will Star remember that it happened? After all, our memories aren't the best.

Star needs to start with recording this information. So, they go to the notes section in their smartphone and type up:

- Bought Equipment, $650, July 1, 2022 from local supplier, Z.

- Signed contract on July 5, 2022 with companies A, B, C, D and E for $1000 each for 2 separate posts. Must all be completed by January 4, 2023.

- Paid lawyer $350 on July 4, 2022 for contract document.

Let's now understand what Star has done. Star has:

- Run a business by doing activities.

- Recorded this information on their phone.

What's the problem?

Well... let's say that the equipment Star purchased was faulty and they want to exchange it.

A note on their phone isn't going to be proof and the local supplier, Z, is pretty busy. They're not going to remember that Star purchased equipment from them. Fortunately, Z is a good operator and they issued Star with an invoice when Star purchased.

The invoice or documentation 🖼 is the proof that Star needs. When you go back and look at Star's business activities, you'll see the 💰 and 🖼 usually together or separately (but there's always some form of 🖼 that goes with the 💰).

So at a basic level, when Star does a business activity that has a 💰 impact, they should record it in their phone but also have the corresponding 🖼. Whether that's the contract, the terms, a receipt, an invoice etc... The proof needs to be there.

At a basic level, when you do business activities you have your proof or evidence from your activity.

This then forms the information for your records. Initially, Star recorded this information in their phone. But, creating invoices in a word processor and keeping notes on your phone isn't organized in a way that's easy to look at. Star will have to use a calculator to add up $650 and $350 to find out how much was spent so far. The calculator gives $940, which means that Star made a typo. This calculating thing isn't really working out for Star. They need a better solution!

This better solution is a system of organization. And this is where the word "accounting system" comes in. It's how you can record and store your information, generate your proof (if you're making a sale) along with getting most of the calculations done without having to type in a bunch of numbers.

If we're going to be really basic—your accounting system is like a refrigerator. In a well-organized refrigerator, you have separate sections for your dairy, meat and vegetables. And the refrigerator also stores the food that comes in until it's taken out and eaten.

An accounting system, when set up properly in different categories, allows you to input in some information to create sales invoices and put them as collaborations, video advertising money etc.... This then gets saved into the system and is then used as part of calculations to show you customized information, like how much in total have you made in sales over the last 6 months.

And how does one get their hands on an accounting system?

By using "accounting software"—a program that can be used to create an accounting system for your business.

This means that Star can stop using the notes on their phone and get accounting software that can help them easily set up an accounting system. This accounting system, Star hopes, will help them manage their business's money better.

So that's how it works.

At a base level, your business will generate activities that have a financial impact, but with these activities, proof should exist alongside.

This proof comes in the form of various documents—a contract, a receipt, an invoice. You need to keep this proof but it doesn't require a closet full of paperwork, a lot of the time, you can keep it in an electronic version like a photo in a secure folder on your computer or cloud storage. But just check that the tax authority in your country or your suppliers will accept electronic documents.

At this point, you have some bills received but nowhere to store them and no system to record sales and create invoices.

This is where your accounting system, enabled by your accounting software, is central to doing all the above and more. Just like the refrigerator is central in storing your food and showing you what's there. Your accounting system, if your software has the capability to, is the central place that records, generates proof in the form of invoices and stores and categorizes the information that's entered so that you can get reports of the information you need later on.

And that's how it all works.

But why?

The key reason is that you, as a business owner, should have information about your business. You should know how much you've made in sales. How much you've spent and after all that, whether your business has anything left behind. This means having the information to make decisions to better manage your business's money and, after all, that's the game in business right?

We know our game now but with every game there are players and that's the second reason.

In running a business, you'll likely need to report to an authority body. And you need to get these numbers correct because shortchanging an authority body might land you in a bit of a bother. So, technically, you're required to keep records and keep them correctly.

Now that you know how it all works, let's learn more about who the players are in your game.

Who's Who?

Knowing your game is important but part of playing your game right is about making sure you know who the other players are, and how to keep them happy.

Why? You might need their help one day and you might have certain obligations to provide them with information.

Now that you know how it all works and how this information is created (remember, record-keeping?), let's introduce the players in the game of business.

Tax Authority

The tax authority is the tax office that rules in your country. In the US, it's the Internal Revenue Service (IRS) and in Australia, it's the Australian Tax Office (ATO).

There's always a lot of concern that comes with tax and for some people, it's the thing they want to avoid most. In fact, some people have said their goal in business is to not pay tax.

This understanding of tax is a bit mistaken. Mainly because tax isn't like a fee that's imposed just for being in business. Tax is a share or slice of what you make.

I like to think of it using the analogy of cake—however, this is a special type of cake, a "business" cake.

Imagine making money in your business as making a cake. Once you have that delicious-smelling cake, people are drawn to the smell. So, once you make money, the tax authority likes to sniff you out (not literally of course!).

The thing is that there's a lot of effort in making a cake. There's the baking, the ingredients, the time spent mixing, the measuring etc.... These things cost money. So once that business cake is created, the first slice that's taken away is to account for the costs involved in making the cake. You'll eat that slice of course!

Now you have cake leftover after taking the first slice out for the spending involved in making the cake.

There's quite a bit leftover so that's great!

But, now... let's say that your housemate, who does all the cleaning in the house, comes into the kitchen where you are, because, well... there's cake.

Your housemate says to you that you need to give them a slice of the cake leftover. But you only need to give them a fifth or 20 per cent. After all... they guilt you by reminding you that they do all the cleaning and if the oven wasn't cleaned, the cake wouldn't have been able to be baked in the first place!

So... you oblige. You don't want to hand them the second slice of cake (you did make it after all and burnt your finger in the process), but you do. Then, your housemate grabs their slice, gobbles it down and leaves the kitchen satisfied.

In this little story, your housemate is the tax authority. They collect their slice (tax) because this slice they collect then gets spent by the government which is generally intended to benefit the public.

The thing is that, for many people, giving a slice of cake is hard. When people go into business with the idea that they don't want to give a slice of cake, what they don't understand is that it's usually against the laws of their country but also, if you don't have a slice of cake to give, that also signifies that you haven't made cake (haven't made any money), and that's a bad thing generally.

No money made. Generally, no tax.

If you've got money left over after accounting for spending in the business (that's generally called profit), you're likely going to have to pay a slice of that to your tax authority.

But, as we know... cake is truly and utterly delicious. So much so that other people also want a slice. And so there are different taxes collected by other authorities that you should be aware of.

The main tax authority generally collects what you call 'income tax'—that's tax from your 'taxable income' which is usually in a very rough conceptual way calculated as the money you make take away the money you spent over a year.

But there's another type of taxation that's generally collected when you invoice or make purchases (usually called sales tax), which will be explored in more detail later on.

As each country and state has their own rules, it's important for you to establish who you have potential tax obligations to so that you meet your obligations and don't get into trouble.

Because if there's anyone you don't want to pick a fight with, it's likely to be a tax authority body!

So, do some research now and consider the following questions:

Who is your main tax authority body:

_____

Any other forms of taxes you might need to pay and to whom?

_____

_____

_____

_____

Are there any key dates or deadlines you need to know for your obligations?

_____

_____

_____

_____

Now, here's a harder question.

How much tax are you supposed to pay and when?

That's a question that requires advice from a suitably qualified professional who can look at your individual situation.

Introducing, the next player in your game...

Accountant

Your accountant is the person you'd generally see to assist you with financial matters - if you need to submit tax forms and report to authority bodies, your accountant should generally be the person you go to for assistance.

And it is good practice to find and establish a good relationship with an accountant or an accounting firm.

Just like having a regular doctor you see who will know your past medical history and manage your health care, establishing a *good* relationship with a *good* accountant can make the financial management part of your business mostly drama-free.

The emphasis is on *good* because having a poor relationship or engaging with an accountant that does not meet your needs or expectations can create problems in your life.

Here are two examples of problematic accountant relationships:

➡ A person whose business was in online marketing had an accountant they saw for six years and thought everything was going swell. They received a letter one day from the tax authority saying that they hadn't submitted their business taxes for the last five years and that they now owed penalties and interest. They tried to get in touch with their accountant because they assumed that their accountant had done all this work—but their accountant became non-responsive. They didn't know what to do because the accountant who they relied on (and paid handsomely) to do this work became the person who created problems for them by not performing the work.

➡ A person was left in limbo without access to all their business's financial information after signing up for a 'client account' in an accounting software, at the recommendation of their accountant. This accountant received an incentive from an accounting software provider for signing up 'client' accounts under their main account. This person signed up and was no longer happy with their accountant and wanted to change accountants. The accountant wanted $1000 to release the person's data to them but the person didn't want to pay. So, they didn't have access to their financial data—the important information they need to report to tax authorities and to understand their business. The irony is that they paid for that data to be entered by their accountant.

What should each person do in the above situations?

Well... if I was the first person, I would compel the existing accountant to provide my financial data and then look for another accountant immediately who had experience in dealing with delinquent tax returns. I would then engage with the new accountant in dealing with the biggest issue first.

The second person is more difficult, because I wouldn't have given complete control to my accountant regarding my financial information in the first place. It's a bad situation though and depending on how much data was there, if I had my proof (remember your documents) and bank statements, I would engage with another accountant to reconstruct my financial data. If the $1000 is more cost-effective, then I'd see if that is a possibility. But, I would get some professional advice on whether the action of withholding data with a release fee of $1,000 is reasonable and allowed under any by-laws that the accountant needed to abide by.

The thing is that the first person didn't know that they could move accountants in the first place—after all, there's a whole lot of setting up and moving to do that's extremely stressful. And the second person never understood fully that their trusted accountant recommended a 'client account' that they had no full control over.

So, what does a *good* relationship with a *good* accountant look like?

Well... it really comes down to your individual needs and expectations but there are some general things to look at. They are:

➡ Qualified. There are various accounting bodies that qualify accountants with a designation. Two examples of a designation would be a Certified Public Accountant (usually registered in a state of the US) and a Chartered Accountant (in Australia and New Zealand). You should check that your accountant holds a qualification with the accounting body in your area.

➡ Experienced in your field of need. Like doctors have different specialization, accountants also have different specializations and areas. If you need a basic tax return done for a small local business, you would not likely engage an accountant specializing in international tax for larger corporations or an accountant who specializes only in audits. If you have any special needs for your work, check to see if they have performed similar work prior to engagement.

➡ Tax preparer or tax agent status. This might come as a shock but not every accountant prepares or can prepare tax returns. If you do require your accountant to communicate with your tax authority or help you with tax matters, then you should check first that they're a tax preparer (in the US) or a tax agent (in Australia). You can search for their name with the body that registers the details of those credentialed to be tax preparers. This is typically the Internal Revenue Service (IRS) in the US and the Tax Practitioners Board (TPB) in Australia.

➡ Enforcement actions or other actions. The accounting board in your area may publish enforcement actions for accountants that have not complied with rules. If they are publicly available, having a quick check to see if the accountant you plan to engage has not been involved in any adverse actions can provide some peace-of-mind.

Beyond the basic things to look at, the relationship itself and how you interact are important. Here are some general tips.

➡ Maintain control. Do not give up complete control of your valuable financial data. With many accounting software and some bank accounts, you'll be able to sign up as the owner of the account but may then invite your accountant as a 'user' of the software or the account. That way, your accountant has access and can perform any needed work but you have control over the account and it belongs to you.

→ Check that things are being done. While your accountant is the person that's supposed to help you and supposed to do the work that you pay them to do, at the end of the day, you are the one responsible for your finances. Check that your accountant has done what you've contracted them to do. For example, if they've sent a tax return, ask if they can send you the paperwork. That way you have a copy of it as proof that it was done.

→ Working in your best interests. If your accountant isn't as responsive as you'd like or for some other reason, you find that the working relationship isn't in your best interests, you may consider leaving the relationship if you're able to without significant legal consequences. Leaving an accountant is not too difficult and generally it involves notifying them and then going through the process of transferring all your financial information and data to your new accountant or to yourself.

→ Do not sign up for marriage – a good working relationship with your accountant should be one that continues because you find their work valuable, not because you're contractually bound for an extended period. It depends on the situation but generally, I tend to avoid long-term contracts for service and focus instead on tasks.

Who knew choosing an accountant was so hard? And not only that, how to interact to work towards a good relationship!

If you want to cut all the hassle of finding an accountant, usefulmoneystuff.com does have a service that sources an accountant for you based on your requirements.

Now, a final word.

The right accountant for you might change over time as your business needs change, so don't be afraid to review your working relationship and move on when it's no longer beneficial or right.

You are the keeper of your business after all.

Write down the details of someone who would be able to help you with your accounting needs:

_____

Let's move on now to the person that does the heavy-lifting with your financial data, the bookkeeper.

Bookkeeper

Managing your finances and doing your accounting is a huge job. There are complicated tasks that come every once in a while and there are routine tasks that need to be regularly completed.

The former is usually done by your accountant while the latter is usually done by a bookkeeper who often works with the accountant.

The bookkeeper is like the kitchen hand to a chef. Their job is to do the record-keeping in your accounting software to keep your financial data up to date with the goings on in your business.

They might create invoices, enter in data from bills received, check to make sure that the transactions in your bank account match with invoices and bills (that's called a bank reconciliation) and a whole lot of record-keeping and data entry work. Depending on their credentials, they may also be able to lodge any quarterly returns or information statements required.

When you have a high volume of documentation, your bookkeeper is the one supposed to help keep your financial record-keeping organized and up-to-date.

Hiring a bookkeeper is again, dependent on your needs.

There are many business owners who don't have a bookkeeper, especially when they're starting out or if they have relatively simple data entry. They often do it themselves and are their own bookkeeper.

And just like an accountant, the working relationship with your bookkeeper, if it is a good one, should be one that is beneficial and relatively drama-free. The general tips for choosing an accountant and interacting with them in the same way also apply to your bookkeeper, if you choose to engage one.

Who's going to do the heavy-lifting with data entry in your business?

Up next is someone who may help keep you on-side with the law (pun intended)...

Lawyer

The lawyer is the all-rounder.

They're the person you'll likely turn to when you need help dealing with a sticky situation, but they can also be the person that helps you get all your paperwork in order so that you don't get yourself in the sticky situation in the first place!

Let's face it—business is about dealing with others and when things go bad, you'll need someone to help you navigate through the legal stuff and find a path out. A good lawyer would be invaluable when it comes to this.

Like an accountant, a lawyer can specialize in certain areas – some may specialize in criminal matters, others may specialize in bankruptcy, some may specialize in taxation, others may specialize in copyright and intellectual property and the list goes on.

This means that when you are engaging the services of a lawyer, you need to be clear on what you want to achieve and the area so that you find a lawyer who is suitably qualified with the right experience to help you. The tips for engagement and maintaining a good working relationship with an accountant also apply with your lawyer.

Usually, in each state, there is a "State Bar" or "Law Society" which has a listing of lawyers with various specializations which may be the first port of call if you are looking for the services of a lawyer.

Who's going to be the person you can turn to when you need help with a sticky situation or want paperwork to keep things in order?

_____

The final player in your game is your bank...

Bank

This final player needs no introduction and if you've ever worked as an employee, you'll have dealt with a bank before.

A bank is a financial institution that lends money and which can accept deposits. As a business person, you'll likely need to deal with a bank when it comes to opening up a bank account where you can deposit money received and pay out monies in the course of your business activities.

But, there may be instances when you might need some money and in such cases, a bank is one place you may go if you want a loan.

Like with all activities, when dealing with a bank, it's important to make sure you read the terms and understand what you are doing.

If you're opening up a bank account, are you aware of any fees that the bank might charge you for keeping your account? If you have a loan, are you aware of your obligations with payments and do you know your interest rate?

And... what happens when you're late with your payments?

When you deal with a bank, the actions that you take can affect your credit score. And missing repayments on your loan can negatively affect this number.

And it's not just actions with the bank, past actions such as bill payment history and other information that affect your credit score can help a lender, like a bank, decide whether or not they'll give you credit or approve a loan. And if you get a loan, this information can be used to decide on an interest rate. The riskier you are, the more likely the interest rate is higher.

Dealing with a bank can be beneficial to you but it's important for you to know the terms you're dealing with so it's a relationship that is best entered into with your eyes wide open —reading the fine print!

What services or products will you use at your bank, if any?

_____

Woah! There are a lot of players in the game of business but knowing how to interact with them and knowing what you can benefit from is important in helping your manage the financials in your business smoothly.

In the next section, we get onto some actions with setting up so you know where to start when managing your business's finances.

3 Steps to Set Up

So far, you've made some key initial decisions, you've learnt how it all (kinda) works and you've learnt about the key players when it comes to managing your business's finances.

Now, it's time to start setting up what you need so that you (or your bookkeeper) can start recording the goings on in your business. Because keeping records means you'll have the information needed about your business to answer those ordinary and also gnarly questions later on.

Let's follow three easy steps to set up.

Step 1 - Open an Account

Opening a bank account is one of the first things you should do when you start a business. But, not any account, it should be a business checking account or a business transaction account. A business checking account is an account where you can receive money but also pay out money. It's set up purely for transactions and that's why it's called a checking account or a transaction account.

And remember, when you set up this account, it should be purely for your business and business use only. Do not mix your personal and business.

Also, because you're starting out in business, look at perhaps signing up for free business checking accounts. Put in "free business bank account" in a web search to see what options are available for you.

Some examples of providers that currently provide free accounts are Bluevine, Relay and Novo in the US and in Australia, NAB, ANZ and Commonwealth Bank are reported to also have no monthly fee business transaction accounts. As institutions do change products from time to time, it is recommended that you do a web search to find out.

Remember, when you're opening a bank account, you're dealing with which player? The bank. Which means that it's important to go in with your eyes wide open and read the fine print to know what you're getting but to also understand when fees and charges may apply.

Once you've decided on a bank account for your needs, you'll need to bring in some paperwork in order for the bank to open your account.

Once that's done, you'll receive an account number and other details for you to receive payments and to make payments out. Most importantly, you would have finished the first step out of the three steps to set up. Well done!

Have you got a dedicated business checking account set up? Make sure you keep your details secure!

Step 2 - Select Accounting Software

Selecting accounting software is an important consideration— after all, this is what you'll be using to record your business's financial information. Your accounting software enables you to create your accounting system—how you'll be recording your bills, invoices and more!

This is also where I've seen people make costly first-timer mistakes, such as:

➡ Using accounting software recommended by their accountant (where the accountant received an incentive) and where the cost of this software was greater than $40 a month. It made up a large chunk of the business's money (as they were only starting out) and it was used only to create less than five invoices a month.

➡ Choosing the most popular software or the one your friend uses, only to find that it costs a lot. You have already entered in a few months of data and now decide to change to a more cost-effective accounting software. Only to have to learn how things work there... and go through the process of transferring your data. Hint! It's not easy as most platforms differ from one another. After wasting a whole week (and money on the other platform) extracting data, transferring data and checking data in your new software, you're finally ready to start recording again. What a hassle it was!

So, why do these problems come about? It comes down to a mismatch of use and cost.

Selecting accounting software is like selecting a refrigerator. In terms of use, you want to make sure it's the right size for your household - too large and it's not going to be used to its full capacity (while using more electricity). Too small and then it won't cater to the needs of the household... which then presents with its own frustrations and headaches. Especially if your household includes young children. And... if you find that the refrigerator you selected isn't going to work out for your household, moving it is a huge, heavy hassle.

When you're starting out, you want to choose accounting software that can cater for your planned usage now, but perhaps for the next three years, if possible. You also want accounting software that is cost-effective. With some accounting software, you do need to 'learn the ropes' on how to do things but the majority of software nowadays comes with a great 'FAQ' or knowledge base where you can search for the answers. It's very different to past accounting software which was mainly used by bookkeepers. Today's accounting software can generally be used by many business owners directly.

To go about this, write down what you need to do in your accounting software. Be very specific—how many invoices do you think you'll receive, how many bills will you need to enter, will you want to import bank statements or do you need them to come in automatically?

Once you've done this, research a few options that match your needs. I would suggest looking at five different options. Then choose the option that best suits you.

There does exist free accounting software and they come in various formats and meet different needs.

Examples of free accounting software just from a web search at the time of this book being published are:

- Manager.io — The desktop edition is free. If using a desktop, you'll need to consider protection of your data such as doing backups.

- Waveapps

- Akaunting

- Zipbooks

- And there are others and new ones on the market.

I personally use a combination of manager.io to perform some tasks and Sage Accounting to do most of my accounting, which is paid cloud accounting software (that means you log into it online, just like if you were to go onto a social media website). For me, it's a very cost-effective accounting software that has met my needs for over five years.

But, with every accounting software, you do need to learn how to do things as creating an invoice in one accounting software may differ slightly from another. Which means that part of your decision-making with selecting accounting software would be to check if the support is to the level that you need. Do you want your emails answered quickly within a time frame or are you happy to go through and find your answer in a knowledge base or FAQ board?

So many things to consider but taking your time to consider all these things will make your life easier. You really don't want to spend time transferring to another software after paying for one software, learning how to use it (which is sometimes a challenge itself) and entering in data.

Take your time to consider carefully what you need, not just now, but for a number of years. Then find options by doing a web search for accounting software that is available and meets your needs. Evaluate them and look at cost—remember, when you're starting out in business (actually, throughout all of business, even established business), you need to monitor your costs. Is the cost of your accounting software going to make up a big chunk of your income or is it reasonable given what you make?

Have you selected your accounting software? Put the details here. Are you aware of how much your accounting software costs? Is this cost reasonable given your business income?

Step 3 - Start Recording

This is the final step of your set up and is the start of a cycle that should continue as long as your business is in existence.

Now that you have your bank account where you'll be able to receive and pay out money from transactions in your business, and you also have your accounting software, where you'll record all these details, you're now set to record the goings on in your business.

Recording is essentially noting down information, not dissimilar to writing down the number of calories in a notebook if you're monitoring what you're eating, or keeping a diary of social events you go to.

Except in financial record keeping, what you're doing is keeping a financial diary. But to make financial information easily accessible when you want to know "how much cash did I have two years ago on this very date", your financial diary isn't in a book form, it's in bits of data (information) that you input in your accounting software.

So, when you're recording your first sale. You might go to the "Create Invoice" section of your accounting software. You might then click "New Invoice" and a form may appear. In this form, you'll input details like customer name, date, details of item being sold, quantity of item being sold, unit price of item being sold and more.

The inputs that you put in are financial information or data that gets stored by your accounting system and can be used later by you to get summarized or individual information about your business.

But it's all there. In one place.

And that's when recording is done right—it means you have a financial representation of the goings on in your business, because you'll need this information for later when your report to tax authorities and most importantly, for yourself, so that you can look back and decide how best to move forward.

As recording is a big area with a lot of considerations, let's move forward now to learn about the basics of keeping your financial diary.

Set Up Your Financial Refrigerator

Have you ever gone to a friend's house and been amazed by how organized they are?

When they open their refrigerator you can see everything clearly laid out. There are dedicated sections in there for vegetables and fruit, meat, dairy and sauces. Everything is in its correct space.

Before they've even purchased anything to go into their refrigerator, they've thought about how to categorize their foodstuffs and where it will go.

That's what you need to do first when it comes to your financial recording keeping. What you'll have are a bunch of bills or receipts or other documentation and notes with information that you'll need to enter into your accounting software.

But before you can enter them in, you need to think about how they're categorized. That is, what type of transaction is this? Kind of like what your friend would do. "Mmm... where should this 🫒 go? Yep, it should go in the fruit section".

But instead of the vegetables and fruit, meat, dairy and sauces, you have four major categories when deciding where your business transactions should be stored when they're recorded. They are:

Revenue / Income

Revenue or Income represents transactions that have earned the business money. For example, if you've sold 50 pots for $1000, that $1000 would be recorded and then stored under the category of "Revenue". Likewise, if you've spent five hours performing cleaning services for a client and you go on your software to create an invoice for $120, the data recorded on the sale of your cleaning hours would be stored under the "Revenue" or "Income" category.

Expense

On the other side of the transaction that receives money into the business from sales, is when the business spends money... in order to make that money in the first place. The spending on things that are used up never to be seen again, like holidays and internet, are called "Expenses".

Let's say a business has a bill for $60 to be paid for internet usage. When this bill is entered into your accounting system, the system should store it under the "Expense" category. That's spending in your business that's being used up. Likewise, if you spend $30 on your accounting software subscription for this month, that too is an expense. You've used it up and need to keep paying to use it next month. If you enter in the details of your accounting software subscription bill to record it in your accounting software, the software should categorize it and store the financial data of that bill under "Expense".

Asset

This is something different, isn't it?

When the business has spent on something like internet, we've seen above that the software, if set up correctly, will store it under the category of "Expense", which means similar items of spending will be under "Expenses".

But, when a business does spend, there is another type of category that it can go under, and that category is "Asset". An asset is something that provides an ongoing benefit to the business (until it's used up) and it's something that's generally kept and that the business can control.

We've established that internet would be an expense. But how about if the business spent money to buy a desktop computer and a comfortable chair?

It's not really used up, right? Because it can be used again and again. And so there needs to be another category to deal with money spent on things that are kept and used for an ongoing period and that category is called "Asset".

And examples of assets are:

➡ Your bank account. The cash in there, if there's any, is something you can use.

➡ The stuff that you buy and resell later, aka inventory or stock. You keep that stuff and don't use it up but it provides you with the benefit of future sales if you manage to sell it.

➡ Property and land.

➡ A fit-out of a room, kitchen etc...

➡ Equipment.

To think of it relating to your organized refrigerator friend, it's like the category of sauce. Unlike vegetables and fruit which have a shorter life span, sauces can be kept for a while and used when needed... until they run out. The sauce that's in a bottle and kept in the fridge...is an asset!

Liability

The last category that a transaction can be stored under when recorded is called "Liability".

You may have heard this word being used before, it usually refers to team members that are underperforming... you know, the sports team member that goes out at night and turns up the next day worse for wear and does badly in training. Or the team member who writes something on social media that brings their team into disrepute. In that way, a liability is seen as something or someone that brings down the overall team value.

With your financial transactions, the liabilities do just that— they bring down the value of the worth of the business because an amount of cash needs to be **paid out sometime in the future**. They are amounts owing, like debt.

Examples of liabilities are:

➡ Trade payables. Bills you've received in the course of doing business but that you haven't yet paid out.

➡ Loans. Because a loan is something you need to pay back and is something you owe, a loan, if you add it into your accounting system, is a liability.

We've now looked at four types of categories under which your financial data can be categorized and stored, but hang on, when you enter in your financial data, like a bill, how on earth does your accounting software know under which category to store it?

That's the next part.

Account Creation

Let's go back to your friend with the organized refrigerator and their avocado. Remember we know that the friend puts the avocado in the compartment of "Vegetables and Fruit" in the refrigerator. If we are going to show this in a skeleton-type format it would be:

‣ Refrigerator

   ‣ Vegetables and Fruit

      ‣ Avocados

   ‣ Meat

- Dairy

- Sauces

Now let's see this same structure applied to an internet bill.

- Accounting software

  - Expenses

    - Internet

  - Revenue

  - Assets

  - Liabilities

So, what you have is an **account** called "Internet" that you set up in your accounting system and with this account, you nominate that it is under the category of "Expenses". This means that when you enter in a bill for internet, it will go into the system and be categorized or "tagged" as an "Expense".

You can really see the power of the accounting system now, can't you? It's your organized friend's refrigerator but for your finances and so much more sophisticated!

But, often accounting software uses codes to represent their account. So internet might be referenced as 201 as you can see in the extended structure below.

- Accounting software

    - Expenses

        - Internet (201)

        - Postage (202)

        - Subscription (203)

    - Revenue

        - Sales (101)

    - Assets

        - Car (301)

    - Liabilities

        - Loan (401)

Those numbers you see: 201, 202, 203, 101, 301, and 401 are accounts and one of the first things you should do in your accounting software is set up a **chart of accounts**.

A chart of accounts is a listing of all the accounts that you'll potentially use to do your record-keeping. Because when you do your record-keeping, you nominate an account to store it in, and then that storage also comes under a category of "Expenses", "Liabilities", "Revenue" or "Assets". And new accounts can be added in later when your business changes.

So with that extended structure above, the **chart of accounts** would look like this:

▸ Internet (201)

▸ Postage (202)

▸ Subscription (203)

▸ Sales (101)

▸ Car (301)

▸ Loan (401)

Why is this important?

Well... think about it....

If you are recording something, say a bill, you need to categorize it in an account so you know what kind of spending it is. If you receive heaps of internet bills, you'll be able to put them in the internet account and see how much you're spending in a month or six months, or a year on internet and that will give you information as to whether to stick with your internet provider or to see more cost-effective options.

It's like having your compartments in the refrigerator. You'll put all your avocados together, but imagine having no section for avocados and putting them randomly in your refrigerator. It would take ages to find and you can't tell if you have too many or too few avocados.

So before you enter data, you need to set up the organizational structure of what group of spending or earning your transaction is. And within that group (say internet), you'd have a further nomination of what type of category it falls under (it would be an expense).

This is a lot to take in because accounting is really about organization and this is advanced level organization that your friend with the organized refrigerator would be proud of.

But, account creation is a fine art—as your friend would agree. Setting up too many accounts might make it over-the-top and confusing for you to track spending and earnings. For example, having two accounts for "Internet" like "Internet fast" and "Internet slow" would be confusing and unnecessary in general. And may also cause confusion when you look at it later on.

While setting up too few accounts might make it hard for you to track later. For example, instead of "Internet", you might have an account called "Communications" where you put all your internet bill records, your telephone bill records and your spending on "PR services". This makes tracking groups of spending harder.

So, it's all about balance when you create your listing of accounts.

Now, onwards to you. You're at the stage now where you're starting your record-keeping and in order to do that, think about the accounts you need right now and potentially in 12 months' time. Write them down as a draft first and write alongside them one of the four categories (asset, liability, revenue, expense) that they belong to.

Then, give yourself some time to think through them and whether their headings are enough for you to understand later on and what documents and transactions the accounts you created represent.

Once you're happy with your listing of accounts, create them in your accounting software.

Write down your accounts here:

Well done! 👍

You've created the backbone of your accounting system, the accounts where you'll store the details of your transaction documents.

Keep Your Proof

Now that you've got your software and within your software, set up accounts that you'll likely need, it's time to consider—what is it that you need to record?

Remember in the "How it Works" section, you saw that in the course of conducting your business, that is, doing the selling and buying of things, these activities had a 💰 impact but with each also came a piece of documentation, or proof 🖼.

It's this proof that you need to record and it's this proof 🖼 that will likely provide you with the **details** that you need to record. It might come in the form of:

▸ Paper-based receipts that you receive when you buy something for the business, in person.

- Regular bills, like those of your email marketing provider, downloaded from your provider's platform for monthly services.

- Contracts for service with your professional consultant or other organization which outline payment schedules and deposits.

- Check received as an up-front deposit by a customer to secure your time for service at an upcoming event.

- An email that confirms specific details of an order being made, with details that confirm the amount to be paid and details for payment.

- Diary entries that confirm the usage of a vehicle for business purposes.

The thing is that proof documents need to be kept as they are the 'backing' or 'receipt' for the records that you'll enter into your accounting system. For example, let's say you've got in your accounting system that you've spent $100 in freight and courier costs. If you're being reviewed and someone (usually the tax authorities) asks you to prove this, it usually comes down to the amount shown in your bank account (going out) and the paperwork you have that shows you did spend this money for that particular purpose.

And the purposes should be for your business, not personal, and for the business in question. Not some unrelated distant business in another far-off field.

Did you also notice that the types of proof can vary? For example, there's an email in there and a check and a regular bill and more.

It's important to note that there are standards in proof. This means that your tax authority might have rules as to what they will accept as proof and what details your proof should contain in order for it to be accepted as a deduction (to reduce your taxable income) or to be considered income.

For example, let's say you purchase a second-hand desk from a stranger after finding it on a classified advertisement website. You don't have documentation but you've got the desk. If you scribble down the amount paid on a piece of paper, would that be enough?

It would unlikely meet the standard for proof because it's just a number scribbled down. More details would likely be needed.

Make sure that the records you keep and store have sufficient detail and that they meet your tax authorities' requirements and some of them can be specific (one tax authority's requirement is the words "Tax Invoice" need to be written on the invoice for claiming of a specific credit)—you might have to consult with your accountant or advisor to assist you in making sure you're meeting the requirements when it comes to your documents.

So how, where and for how long do you keep your proof?

You can keep your proof in a range of ways—but the common ways are in physical paper format, in electronic format or a hybrid of both. And in terms of where, it should be somewhere you choose that is secure. It is precious information after all.

I personally like to keep my proof in electronic format. Most of my proof such as bills and invoices come via email in PDF format and I transfer this into a secure cloud folder. If they are in paper format, I'll take photos of them on my phone and upload them in the image file type of "PNG" or "JPG" into the same secure cloud folder. I'll back up this folder so that in the instance of an issue, I still have a copy of it.

See, all my proof is in the one place and ready to be entered into the accounting system. Too easy!

The other issue is how to store your proof.

And a way to think about how to store it is to consider yourself in a year's time when you need to find a particular piece of proof for a refund dispute.

How will you find it?

If you've put all your proof in a suitcase, you might find it takes hours or days to look for it. Likewise, if you named your proof "589065.png", you might be searching through electronic file after electronic file to look for it.

So how you store your proof matters—if you want to avoid spending days going on a treasure hunt!

Let's say you had stored this proof as:

▸ 20210701-invoice-james-2548.pdf

So you have a "PDF" file type and just from its name you can see that it was created in 2021 in July on the first day of that month. You can see it was an invoice, which means you made a sale to a customer called "James" for the amount of 2548.

This will allow you to search for the document either nested in monthly folders or by using the search function on your computer (if you have one) to look for certain words like "James", "2548" or "202107".

Too easy right? And you've saved yourself hours and days from looking up a random document with no easily discernible name.

The way you name your files (if electronic) and how you store your physical files (in folders) will make it easier to retrieve them if you need to later on.

Finally, how long do you need to store all your proof?

The IRS (in the US) and the ATO (in Australia) all have guidance as to record-keeping requirements and the length of time you're supposed to retain records, and we would recommend doing a web search to look for the most recent guidance from your relevant tax authority to check the length of time. But there are instances, usually in other legislation, where you might be required to retain records for an indefinite period of time.

There is general guidance that seven years is a good length of time to keep records. However, I like to keep mine indefinitely.

This is because you don't know what the future holds, but it's also for a practical reason. Electronic files don't take up much physical space and so it's not difficult or a hassle to keep my records indefinitely. After all, you never know if you'll receive an enquiry relating to something that's 15 years old!

The key with your proof is that you should store it in a way that's secure, easily accessible by you and easily retrievable by you, in the instance that you need to access it.

How will you store your proof documents?

Regular Dates

Keeping records isn't just a once-off, it's an ongoing process that you need to commit to on a regular basis. Why? Well, a business continually does activities which will generate proof documents that you'll need to record. It's simple as that!

If you leave your records to pile up, you may miss important information and when you actually come to do your records, you'll find it to be a larger and longer process.

So, it's important to set a date that occurs at a regular interval for you to sit down and put your records in your accounting system.

It could be daily, weekly, fortnightly, monthly, quarterly... but it depends on what your needs are. If you have a lot of volume with transactions, you might need to do your record-keeping weekly. If you have records that are being tracked by another system, you might be able to do your record-keeping monthly or quarterly and extract that information from your other system when the time comes.

I do my record-keeping quarterly, just because I need to report to the tax authority quarterly. But, then I record sales daily in a separate system, just to keep track and address any issues as they come quickly. And if sales do not come in via the automated system, I would then access the system to create an invoice (and that creates the sales data as well) on an as-needs basis.

You need to find out what frequency works for you—and the frequency might change with time and as your business changes. But the most important thing is to schedule in your dates and commit to doing so because if you don't, it creates additional work (usually working backwards to sort through piles of paperwork) that could be better spent doing something else... like enjoying a piece of cake!

The more frequently the records are done, the more up-to-date information you have. But you need to balance this with what your business needs are and what you can realistically commit to.

How frequently will you do your records? Have you scheduled in your dates yet? Write down your plans here:

_____

_____

_____

_____

_____

Enter Data

This is the action part of managing your business's finances if there ever were to be one!

If your idea of a good night out is a cup of tea and listening to public radio, you'll be in good company considering this "action". For most other people, this action will probably be considered pretty tame.

Grab a chair, and open your accounting software, have your proof handy—it's now time to enter in your records.

Ins and Outs

The first thing to decide when entering in data is where to enter it, and part of that means determining if your proof document represents an "in" or an "out" in the business.

An "in" means that the proof document relates to money that comes into your business.

An "out" means that the proof document relates to money that comes out of your business.

If it's an "in" document, depending on how your accounting software is set up and how they name things, the section that you'll likely go to enter in documents relating to "ins" would be "Invoices", "Earnings" or "Sales".

Let's say you receive a compensation report for a self-publishing book company that outlines the sales you made and how much they're going to deposit in your bank account. At this stage, you haven't sent them an invoice but they've reported to you so this is the proof that you need for your recording. Because that's money that you're set to receive.

This is an "in" document, so you'd record this in your sales/invoices section so that information can stay in your accounting system. You don't necessarily need to send them the invoice as they've already done the calculations for you but you still need to record the data in your accounting software—this is so you have this information in the one spot when you need to pull up information and ask "How much money did my business make in total?"

Now, let's consider the "out" documents. Again, depending on how your accounting software is set up and their names for section, the section where you'd likely go to enter in documents related to the "outs" in your business would be "Purchases", "Spending" or "Bills".

Let's say you've received a bill from your internet provider and you've stored it in your online folder and have it opened in front of you on the computer to enter in the details. You'd go to the section that records bills or purchases and enter in all the relevant details. Remember, bills do differ from one another and you'd fill in the details from your bill into the accounting software to record that one bill. This means that you've recorded that money is supposed to go "out" of your business and later, you'll be able to match this record to the money that goes out in your bank statement (that matching activity is called a "bank reconciliation").

Then there are other proof documents that might function as an "in" or an "out" document depending on what's described on there. And ones that don't necessarily need entering in, but provide proof of something happening. For example, let's say you receive a bill for a desk two weeks ago, but you've only paid them today and received a receipt for your payment of the bill.

In this case, the receipt acts as an "out" document but, it is proof of payment for your bill that was originally entered into the system. You wouldn't record the receipt again as spending but rather, when you do that matching activity (where you match your record with your bank statement—we cover this in the next chapter called "Check It"), you'll upload or keep that receipt aside, just as proof of payment.

So that's the first part, knowing where in your accounting system you're supposed to record your proof documents or business transactions.

Let's now move onto the next step-that's filling in the details once you've got your form up.

Dates

Let's start with something easy. One of the details you'll enter into your form whether it is for sales or purchases would be the date.

It's important you select the right date on your form when you enter in data for reasons being that if you put in the wrong date, when you go to reference the data again, it might not show up. For example, if you want to pull up all the purchases you've spent in one month but you mistakenly entered in the date using the two months ago, your reported information will be missing that crucial part.

Also, just be careful you don't put in the incorrect date. For example, if you receive a bill and the bill is dated the first of this month, but also has a due date at the end of the following month, you'd put down the bill date (first of this month).

If you put down the due date for payment as the bill date in your records, it would mean that the information isn't being reflected correctly...which means problems in reworking and fixing things later for you (or your bookkeeper).

That's the date addressed now. The next part is addressing what's been purchased or what's been earned.

Account

This part is where the accounts that you created (back in the section "Account Creation") are used. When you created an account in your listing of accounts, you essentially created an invisible "holding bay". This holding bay is where bills or invoices that meet your account criteria can be stored.

So, let's say you have an account called "Internet"—the invoices that would belong there would be bills relating to spending on internet access. You wouldn't include bills relating to other things.

When you create your record of a purchase or sale, you're going to nominate the account that this purchase or sale will be "stored" under and how you decide that depends on what the item is that's being purchased or sold.

You'll write a quick description of what's been sold or purchased (like Monthly Internet) and then select the "Account" (the Internet account that you created) to which you want this record to be "stored".

In some larger companies, they do this beforehand where a division manager might have the bills on their desk and they'll write down a number "483" which may represent a code for the "Postage" account. This action of itemizing shows where the records of this bill is supposed to be stored. This bill then gets sent to the accounts department and they enter this bill in their system and they'll itemize it into the "483" account which for them, is the postage account. This account holds all the bills that relate to postage.

Now... it's all coming together.

Stock / Inventory Management

Some businesses buy items for the purpose of selling those items that were originally bought. For example, a homeware retailer that buys homewares from various suppliers at wholesale prices and then puts the items in their warehouse to sell to the public, has inventory or stock. The inventory or stock are the items that they buy and hold (even if it's for a short period of time) for subsequent sale.

If your business does this, it likely has inventory and you might find this section useful. If your business doesn't have inventory, then feel free to skip this section.

Inventory is usually dealt with in a separate section of your accounting software and this is because there's quite a bit to managing inventory. You need to usually keep track of the different types of inventory items you have, how much you have left, how much it cost and how much you sold them for.

If you're entering data and have inventory as part of your business, then check whether your accounting software has a separate section for managing inventory or stock.

If they do, then set up an inventory item. This is the item that you're going to be buying and selling. For example, let's say you buy and sell pet beds through an online marketplace.

You'd go to your inventory item page and set up your inventory items by filling in a form.

It might look like this:

Item code	Name	Purchase price	Sales Price	Description	Starting Balance
DB2	Dog bed blue	15	59	Blue dog bed medium	0
CB1	Cat bed blue	15	59	Blue cat bed small	2

This means you buy and sell two items. One being a blue dog bed in a medium size and another a blue cat bed in a small size. You've given each a code (so it's easier than typing the full name and it's easier to nominate when it comes to record-keeping). For each of the beds, their purchase price (the price you pay to buy them) is $15 and you sell them for $59 each. You've also got two already on hand with you of CB1 and none of DB2.

This part just sets up what you have so far and inputs it into the system so that you can use it later.

So what happens with the record-keeping now when you actually buy or sell your inventory items?

Well... it's similar to the previous sections. You'll need to decide on the ins and outs and then nominate an account—however, because you have inventory, it's managed slightly differently.

Let's look at what happens when it's an "in".

If it's an "in" transaction, that means you're selling inventory to bring money into the business. So you'd go to your sales or invoices section in your accounting software. There's nothing new there.

You'd click on the button and fill in the standard details. When it comes to the description section where you'd normally nominate your account where the record would be stored, you'd instead nominate "Item" or something similar (as accounting software can have different names for things).

When you click "Item", you typically should see one of the inventory item codes that you set up. Then you'd select the code of the inventory item that you're selling. What this generally does (depending on your accounting software) is that it nominates the account automatically being "Inventory Sales" (under revenue) and at the same time, it reduces the inventory held (asset) account as you're moving your inventory from being held by you to being taken out and sold.

What happens when it's an "out" transaction?

Similar thing. You'd go to your purchases or spending section and create a purchase invoice (to replicate the details of the purchase invoice you would have received from your supplier into your accounting system). Instead of clicking account, you'd select the "Item" that you purchased from the dropdown. What this does is adds the number of items you purchased into your inventory account (this is usually a system set up for you when you set up your inventory items).

So that's inventory. It's usually a separate section in your accounting system but once you set it up, you'd use your "Items" rather than nominate an account (as that's typically done automatically for you when you have accounting software with a separate inventory section) when you're buying or selling inventory.

This helps the system keep track of how much inventory you have but it may also provide valuable information as to what inventory lines are providing the best "bang for your buck!"

Let's move onto the next part of entering in data and that's considering the quantity and the price.

Quantity and Unit Price

At a basic level, when you create your record in your accounting software for your bill or invoice, you should record it at its smallest unit level.

What does this mean?

It means that an invoice or bill usually has a total but that total is made up of smaller parts—it's these smaller parts that you should record to make up the total.

Let's use the example of a babysitter that invoices a family for $1,000 for the week. That total is made up of smaller parts, let's say:

▸ Hours babysitting totaling $800

▸ Hours doing miscellaneous housework $200

But there are smaller parts than that:

▸ The babysitter spent 32 hours that week babysitting and they charge $25 an hour.

▸ The babysitter did five hours of cleaning charging $30 an hour and they also did some basic food preparation (five hours worth) that they charged at $10 an hour.

These are the smaller parts that you would record as line items when recording your bill or invoice. They're called line items as they're each on separate lines and you do want to record in this level of detail because you might need to reference it later on. For example, in the instance with the babysitter, the family might wonder why they've been charged $200 in extra services and breaking it down for them can make it easier for them to understand (or dispute).

Actually, I have heard of people who don't put too much detail in their invoices because when they did, people would start disputing how much things individually cost—so they would put the detail in their record keeping, but the invoice they issued to their customer was modified to remove too much detail.

So, in the instance of the babysitter, what is being sold?

It's their time, by the hour. This is what you consider the item. But there are also three different types of items. They are: time cleaning, time doing food preparation and time babysitting.

Within these three items you have the quantity, that means the total number of items. So if the item is time by the hour, that means how many hours.

And the unit price is the price charged per hour. Once you multiply the unit price with the quantity for each line item and then add the totals, you get the full total of $1,000.

This is how it would look (depending on your accounting software) in the Item or Description part of your records for your invoice or bill:

Description

Item	Quantity	Unit Price	Total
Babysitting hours	32	25	800
Cleaning hours	5	30	150
Food preparation hours	5	10	50
Total			1000

So remember, when record-keeping, put in the basic level of detail so that you have this to refer to later. The quantity is the number of the basic unit that you're selling or purchasing. The unit price is the cost or the sales price for one unit of the item.

You've nearly completed most of your entry for a record now and there was a lot to learn, so nice work!

The next section is about taxation because depending on where you're doing business, you might have to collect taxes for your sales or pay taxes when purchasing. This information, where appropriate, should be captured in your accounting system.

Taxation

Earlier on we spoke about taxation and likened it to the second slice of the "business" cake being taken away, where the original cake represented your total earnings and the first slice taken away was to take away the costs involved in making it.

This was income taxation.

It's taxation on the taxable income (that's usually total revenue take away spending to create that revenue, but the calculation is more specific and should be done by an accountant for your specific situation).

Income taxation is usually done at the end of the year and is filed to the federal tax authority.

There is another type of taxation that your business might have to account for and we mentioned this briefly before.

Let's say you go to a shop and you buy a heated pizza slice and you want to take it home to eat. You pay for the pizza and you get a receipt. On that receipt, it shows the amount you paid, but you look more closely.... That amount you paid is made up of your "pizza" amount but also includes amounts of tax that the shop has to collect for other authorities whether local, state or other.

You've paid a certain type of taxation at the point of your purchase and the shop has collected taxation from you at the point of sale.

This taxation is one that you usually collect when you make a sale or is collected from you when you buy something. We'll call it sales taxation in this book but it's also known by other names depending on your location, such as GST, VAT, withholding etc...

Going back to the cake anecdote, income taxation was the second slice of cake taken away after there was left over cake.

Sales taxation is a different beast.

It's not part of your "sales" but it's an amount you collect in addition, as part of making a sale. Kind of like saying that if you make a cake, you also need to make cupcakes in addition to the cake. And a different type of authority will take those cupcakes away—thank you very much!

It's this type of taxation that should be recorded in your accounting system when you go to record your bills or invoices. It's not end-of-year taxation (typically income tax), it's taxation as you go about your business (sales tax).

Before we go further, this book looks at taxation for general information and no part of this book is considered taxation advice.

Here's where sales taxation gets tricky.

This type of taxation can go by various names like sales tax, consumption tax, value-added tax, or goods and services tax and can have certain rules. Such rules are that you might have to register in order to collect the tax and this particular tax might apply to certain items a business sells and may not apply to others. It can be set by state authorities, local authorities or both or another body and the rates vary depending on where you're doing business and a whole range of other factors.

Because it can be tricky, it is highly recommended that you seek advice from a qualified professional for your situation in order to understand what you need to do to meet any sales or consumption tax requirements, from the outset. And then you can follow their advice going forward. Sometimes, it might just be to establish what you need to do with taxation for your sales so you know upfront and then can apply the appropriate rate or rates.

We do recommend doing this at the beginning rather than later because if you do your consumption or sales taxes incorrectly, you could potentially be penalized or be charged interest. That level of stress is best avoided by establishing what you need to do upfront to meet your sales tax requirement and then doing it!

At usefulmoneystuff.com, there is a service which finds you an advisor to help you with this stuff, if you wish to have someone do the hard work, and can search for someone with the right qualifications to help you.

It's also important to note that within some accounting software, there is guidance with sales tax and rates that are applicable which may be helpful to you when it comes to recording.

But one of the things you do need to know when it comes to taxes that are collected on sales is the concept of exclusive or inclusive as it will most likely appear in your accounting software.

The words "inclusive" or "exclusive" signal to your accounting software whether to:

▸ Add the sales tax on top of your total figures (exclusive), or

▸ Calculate the portion of your total figures that would be the tax part (inclusive).

While they're simple, it's important to get the nomination right, just so that your system is correctly calculating the amount of taxation.

Let's go back to the example of the babysitter. Remember that the babysitter wanted to charge $1000.

If the babysitter does have to collect sales taxes, and let's say these sale taxes are 10% of sales, they'll have to nominate "inclusive" or "exclusive" when entering in their invoice.

If the babysitter nominates "exclusive" - that means that the accounting software will add 10% to the final price charged to the customer which means that the total invoice would look like this.

Description

Item	Quantity	Unit Price	Total
Babysitting hours	32	25	800
Cleaning hours	5	30	150
Food preparation hours	5	10	50
Subtotal			1000
Sales tax (10%)			100
Total			1100

This means that the customer pays $1100 and the babysitter will receive $1000 but the babysitter has collected $100 that they'll send to the comptroller or other tax authority to whom they need to report, specifically for sales tax.

How about if the babysitter nominated "inclusive"?

In that case, most accounting systems would take the $1000 after the total amount including sales tax and so would calculate a before tax amount and the tax amount.

Description

Item	Quantity	Unit Price	Total
Babysitting hours	32	25	800
Cleaning hours	5	30	150
Food preparation hours	5	10	50
Before Sales Tax			909.09
Includes sales tax (10%)			90.91
Total			1000

This means that the customer pays $1000 and the babysitter will only get $909.09 and they'll collect $90.91 to be given to the tax authority.

You'll also notice that each line total: 800, 150 and 50 do not add to 909.09. They add to 1000, which is the final total and the 800, 150 and 50 are considered by the accounting system (when you nominate "inclusive") to include the 10% tax within those figures.

The babysitter may not be happy with receiving $909.09 and giving $90.81. They really wanted the full $1000 and then the $100 to be collected on top and given to the tax authority. So it's important to check totals to make sure you're using "exclusive" or "inclusive" properly. You don't want to shortchange yourself, do you?

So where does this sales tax go in your records after you've say, created an invoice?

Well... usually in accounting software, it will go into a "system account". Remember how you created a list of accounts for your record-keeping? Generally, accounting software will have their own generated accounts that are used by the system.

This sales tax account stores the sales tax amounts that are collected or paid as you go about your record-keeping and then at the end of a certain period, let's say, a month, you'll be able to check the sales tax account to see how much altogether you owe or should be refunded from your tax authority (if they offer credits for sales taxes on your purchases).

Well done! You've gotten to the end of the "Enter Data" part and after this, you should be on your way to entering data and creating those records for all the activities in your business. Remember the ins and outs and, once you decide that, the other details get inputted in the form and there it is... a record that hits your account!

And you don't just enter data once, you enter data as part of running a business. It's part of the parcel!

But, unfortunately, that's not the end.

Remember, when you create an invoice or add in a bill, it records that you've made a sale or made a purchase. It doesn't say that it's been paid...

And that brings us onto the final part. The all-important check to make sure that your sales have been paid and you've paid your purchases.

Check It

To You,

In the most recent filing you lodged with us, it has come to our attention that you have underpaid your taxes. Please make sure you pay $90,000 by the deadline. A penalty of $25,000 applies.

From: An authority you don't want to mess with.

Nope—This is not a hoax email (although it sounds very much like one). It's what can potentially happen to you if you fail to check the accuracy of your records.

The information that you enter in your accounting system generates your data—this is the data that you, anyone who assists you and the authorities will rely on for important things like filings and reports.

So, that means that it has to be as correct as it could possibly be.

Errors made in your recording, like accidentally typing a smaller sales number and sending your invoice, may lead to unintended and bad situations such as underreporting of sales tax. And you don't want to do something like this because penalties and/or interest could then apply. Even if it was just 'a mistake'.

And it's not only the tax authorities that might come knocking. It's you that might have to take a financial hit to your business if what you delivered was well and truly more than the 'mistake' invoice total amount and your customer later paid the 'mistake' invoice and considered it as a 'done deal'.

One small mistake can have so many unintended and bad financial consequences.

But... accidents do happen with record-keeping so it's important to be able to pick up on these mistakes.

How do you do that?

First, do a check prior to saving your invoices or bills and a secondary check prior to sending any invoices. Check for:

▸ Total amount—does this match up with any other documents e.g. contracts or written communications?

▸ Description—ensure that all your details are correct and you're not promising something that wasn't agreed to or underdelivering.

▸ Dates—they're so simple that it's easy to overlook them and get the date wrong. But, writing a due date for next year isn't going to be in your best interests. Make sure you check your dates as they can affect the timing of taxation obligations.

▸ Account—when setting up your account, make sure it belongs in the right category. Incorrect set ups with choosing one of the four categories can affect your income tax (the one usually done at the end of the year). Additionally, it's important to select the right account. You don't want to select the "sales" account when you were supposed to record a bill because that could be mistaken for a refund... and then those unintended bad situations might come about.

They're just basic checks you want to do when you do your records.

But there's a huge check that should be done that really completes your record-keeping, and that check is called a bank reconciliation.

When you entered in your records in your accounting system, that is, took out your bills and then copied down the details so that the information could be recorded in your software or created an invoice that would store the sales details in your software—you were only doing one side of the full transaction.

You recorded that there was a bill (money owing to someone else) and a sale (money owing to you from someone else)...

But in your system, you didn't record the payment.

That's the actual money that flows into your bank account from a sale or the money that comes out of your bank account when you pay your bills.

So the missing part to make sure that invoices are being paid (and match up to amounts) and that bills are paid for their total amounts, is a check that matches up the individual transaction line in your bank statement to the invoice or bill that you recorded in your accounting system.

So you did PART 1: Enter in data for your business activities.

You now need to do PART 2: Match up your data with your bank transactions.

Once you do Part 2, you've got a full transaction that's complete in your accounting system. Awesome right?

Let's get into the nitty gritty now as to how you can do your bank reconciliation because, just from the outset, thinking about printing out your bank statement and manually going through each line (there could be hundreds) and ticking them off as you find the matching invoice or bill sounds extremely tedious.

It is tedious work but time-saving later on. And using accounting software can make your life easier here.

So, let's see how to do Part 2.

Bank Reconciliation

The first part of doing your bank reconciliation is determining how to do it.

You can do it manually and, in such a case, you'd have the printed out version of your bank statement and individually go through each line and tick off each line once you matched it up to an invoice or bill recorded in your software. You'd also have a reference label that you'd write down next to each bank statement line so that you could easily locate the invoice or bill later if you had to.

Your bank statement might look like this (and remember, bank statements from different banks might look different):

Deposits and other credits

Date	Description	Amount
Jul 8, 2022	#012 Deposit J Tay	59.99
Jul 19, 2022	#048 Deposit K Rowe	59.99
Total deposits and other credits		**$119.98**

Withdrawals and other debits

Date	Description	Amount
Jul 2, 2022	Trn: 2902 Toys Supplier	51.98
Jul 28, 2022	Trn: 9348 Internet	60
Jul 28, 2022	Trn: 3849 Equip Rental	50
Total withdrawals and other debits		**$161.98**

Service fees

Date	Description	Amount
Jul 31, 2022	Transfer fees	10
Total service fees		

Daily ledger balances

Date	Balance ($)
Jul 1, 2022	804
Jul 2, 2022	752.02
Jul 8, 2022	812.01
Jul 19, 2022	872
Jul 28, 2022	762
Jul 31, 2022	752

There's quite a bit of information there but let's say I've gone through each line and attempted to match them up with my records and I wrote notes on the bank statement (underlined). This is my bank reconciliation being done. Let's see what it looks like:

Deposits and other credits

Date	Description	Amount	
Jul 8, 2022	#012 Deposit J Tay	59.99	Checked. Inv #57
Jul 19, 2022	#048 Deposit K Rowe	59.99	No invoice. Issue please.
Total deposits and other credits		**$119.98**	

Withdrawals and other debits

Date	Description	Amount	
Jul 2, 2022	Trn: 2902 Toys Supplier	51.98	Checked. Bill #98
Jul 28, 2022	Trn: 9348 Internet	60	Bill #6754 from TG was $50 forgot to pay discounted amount.
Jul 28, 2022	Trn: 3849 Equip Rental	50	Checked. Bill #584 from ER
Total withdrawals and other debits		**$161.98**	

Service fees

Date	Description	Amount	
Jul 31, 2022	Transfer fees	10	Valid charge. Bank terms.
Total service fees		**$10**	

Daily ledger balances

Date	Balance ($)
Jul 1, 2022	804
Jul 2, 2022	752.02
Jul 8, 2022	812.01
Jul 19, 2022	872
Jul 28, 2022	762
Jul 31, 2022	752

Bank rec done Jul 31, 2022
signed by VN

So, there you are... an old-school manual bank reconciliation. You'll see that it's a check of each line in the bank statement and a check of whether it matches up with a bill or invoice.

But is that all a bank reconciliation is? A check and once you've written down the notes, it's done?

No. It's a check and where there is an inconsistency, to create action to complete. Actions coming from the above bank reconciliation are:

▸ To create an invoice as K Rowe paid and received their item but the owner forgot to create and send K Rowe their invoice. So, they should do it now and then it can be matched and that particular section can be updated to say "Checked" with the invoice number.

- ‣ Email TG to confirm that you have a credit because you overpaid by $10 in "Trn: 9348 Internet". Then use this credit next time you pay.

Once it has been actioned, I'd also write a note after the existing "Bank rec done Jul 31, 2022 signed by VN" note to provide an update as to what had been done. This helps you track back later when something's amiss.

You'll also notice something else...

In the service fees, you'll see an amount of $10. In the notes, you'll also see "Valid charge. Bank Terms". This means that the amount of $10 is a valid charge by the bank based on their terms—which are usually provided to you when you open your account. It's unlikely that they'll issue you an invoice when your service fees are charged. They're just directly taken from your account.

In this instance, you have an amount in your bank statement of $10 going out but no bill. It does still need to be entered into your accounting software and a lot of accounting software allows you to create an entry to store this $10 transaction somewhere as a cash out transaction.

So what you'd do in your accounting software is allocate your bank fees to a "Bank Fees" or similar account and put in the other details like tax, if any. When you press "Save" or something similar, it creates that record in your accounting system of $10 in cash that went to pay "Bank Fees" without an invoice.

Isn't that neat?

A bank reconciliation can make our record-keeping more complete because there can be items that are charged or paid out of our bank account which no invoice or bill relates to. But if they're a valid spend or earning, then you'll be able to record them in your system.

That's a bank reconciliation for you—the old-school way but with all the concepts and checks that are still relevant today.

And how does someone perform a bank reconciliation, not manually, but by using their software?

The process (checking for a match and if not, looking into it further) is still the same but the major difference is importing your bank statement or the bank transaction into your accounting software.

A lot of accounting software would have a specific section for your bank account and the importing of your bank transactions.

You would set up a "bank account" section in your accounting software that would mimic what you have in your bank account. Depending on your software, you might be able to get "bank feeds" (sometimes daily)—that's where the bank transactions feed directly into the bank section of your accounting software so that you can match them up and do your bank reconciliation via the software.

Otherwise, you may have to import (this is what I do). If importing, decide on a time period, let's say we'll import last month's bank transactions at the beginning of each month. Then it's a matter of working with your bank's software to extract a file type that your accounting system can work with. There are many different file types and your accounting software FAQ is the best place to get information about which file types they accept. I usually work with a QIF file. I set date parameters, extract the data from my online banking and then import it into my accounting software.

From here, you can electronically do a bank reconciliation where you match up invoices, bills, create records directly from the bank transactions in your system (if they're valid) and query transactions if there are any inconsistencies.

Just like keeping records, a bank reconciliation is also an ongoing process. It can't be done just once but it is considered part of the ongoing record-keeping process. After all, you can't have incomplete records, right? And a bank reconciliation is that final part which helps to minimize missing records and to tie your record-keeping all together.

Because this section did cover quite a bit, let's summarize!

With a bank reconciliation:

▸ You'll need a bank statement. If you're doing it manually, the old-school way, the paper statement. If you're doing it electronically, which is how it's generally done nowadays, you'll need to organize bank feeds or set up a regular period where you'll commit to extracting your bank transactions for a set time period and importing them into your accounting software.

▸ Then you match up and create accounts and complete any actions for loose ends.

There you have it... the final (but ongoing part) of keeping records.

You've Got Records

By now you should be starting to get the hang of the accounting process of record-keeping that continues alongside your business activities, replicating them into an accounting system so that you can get financial information about your business when you need it.

It really is an ongoing process where you: enter data, do your bank reconciliation, address any inconsistencies, enter data, do your bank reconciliation, address any inconsistencies... and you get the drift.

Once you've gotten the hang of it, you've got records. But is that it?

No, having records means having the crucial financial information you need to do a whole range of tasks related to running a business.

You then have to use that information to take action and manage your business effectively, just like the boss that you are!

Manage Your Business Like a Boss

Let's get into the next phase now and that's using the information you've recorded to start getting into some good habits that help you manage your business's money better.

In this section, you'll look at some simple activities that you can do yourself (or with your accountant or bookkeeper) on a regular basis to help keep your finances well managed.

Problems that occur with the financial management of a business can occur at anytime and how they can come about can be different for each business person.

Even if you have the best record-keeping, if you don't further manage, problems can still happen, causing you pain and stress.

Such problems are not having enough cash on hand to pay your bills, even if you've had a great month of sales. How can that happen? Credit sales. If you don't collect the cash on your credit sales within a reasonable timeframe, you won't have cash to pay your bills. And cue the headaches and desperate phone calls...

How about having quite a bit of cash on hand but making heaps of purchases and not knowing who you have to pay first? If you keep missing bill payments, your supplier might just start questioning whether they would want to continue working with your business.

And then there are issues with moving inventory. Let's say you buy and sell clothes but don't manage your stock holdings properly so you're not getting rid of 'out-of-style' clothes. What might happen is that those clothes may just stay there in your warehouse unable to be sold, or slowly, they're being eaten by moths. They're not just clothes, they're money you borrowed and you spent (let's say $50,000) that's left to dwindle. Some problems may not immediately look like problems because they happen so slowly, but they leave a big hole in your finances.

Then there are the problems that are obvious, not straight away, but have been left to fester for months or years and they become big problems that hit you in one go with... the dreaded authority letter.

This is the one that often creates a lot of stress for people. Mainly because it usually relates to a large sum of money, people thought it was addressed and they don't really know how to deal with it because it's become complex and usually requires digging back. When the letter also includes penalties and interest... well, that just adds to the stress felt.

The thing is that many of these problems can be avoided by managing your business properly. You've got the record-keeping part of it now, it's time to take action to use that information (by accessing the "Reports" section in your accounting software) to do things to keep your business on track.

It's like keeping a household running. You continually have to buy food, do the cleaning, address problems immediately as they arise and other little jobs to make sure your household runs optimally. Neglect this, and it takes longer to 'fix up' and you've got a household that 'needs a little work'.

Let's see how you can keep a happy household with your business by considering four areas.

Collecting Payments

The first section is about collecting payments. And for some reason, a lot of people feel uncomfortable about doing this. It makes them feel like a debt collector or just gross. Especially, when the customer on the other end is saying that they should "Relax, and I'll pay you soon! Geez... 😊" and the payment never comes... this is after they were happy to use your services... and enquired recently whether they could use your services again...

When someone buys from you on credit or they haven't yet paid, they owe you a debt. And you have to receive it. That's why, in the accounting world, the money that you're set to receive is called a receivable.

One of the reports that your accounting software may generate is called an "Aged Receivables" report or a name that is similar. That report shows you the receivables that are still outstanding and due to be paid to you and by how many days.

So what do you do after you know about this?

Well... you need to follow up.

And for many businesses, the standard way to follow up is to send the customer a statement (you should be able to find out where in your accounting software your "customer statements" are to extra) with a simple message saying:

Dear [Customer Name],

Your account is now overdue and your customer statement attached. Please make arrangements to settle outstanding amounts owing to us as soon as possible.

Kind regards,

[Business name].

Simple and easy right? And, did you know that may also help to protect you?

When you don't follow up on a debt, especially after a long time, it may be perceived that you have "forgiven" their debt i.e. saying "it's okay, you don't need to pay me", or it can be seen as modifying the contract of sale you had with the customer.

After all, it's your actions that show your intentions.

That's why it's super important that you follow up on amounts owing to say that they need to pay so that if it comes to the point where you have to go the legal route, you'll have your documents saying that you did try to chase up on the payments and that they're owing to you.

The other question is what happens after?

Well... the best outcome is that they pay their bill and you get your money. You do your bank reconciliation and that invoice is marked off as paid. Other outcomes depend on how the situation unfolds. In the past, after say three follow ups, I've seen a renegotiation of pricing, referral of the debt to a debt collector and/or proceeding of the claim to a claims court. Usually, when that happens it becomes more complicated and you'd call on your attorney or solicitor to assist as each situation is unique.

But in terms of keeping your business on track with collecting payments, make sure you schedule a regular interval, depending on your business needs, it could be weekly, monthly etc... so that you know what receivables are outstanding and that you're following up on them appropriately.

After all, you provide your customers with a valuable service or product, and they are obliged to pay you the amount owing. It is not gross to want them to pay up and it's certainly not unreasonable to keep them accountable to their promise to pay. You've kept your end of the bargain, they should too!

Bills to Pay

On the flip side, let's now consider payables. They're amounts that you're supposed to pay others. Somewhere along the line your purchased things for the business but didn't pay up front. You've got the purchase invoice or bill but haven't paid. This means you have a debt to whomever you purchased from.

Similar to aged receivables, you want to regularly run a report, usually called the "Aged Payables" report to know which bills you still need to pay. And when you should pay them (please pay by the due date).

All you have to do once you've identified who needs payment is to check the invoice and make sure it's valid and the details are correct, and then make payment.

This one's really simple. You don't want to be the person that others are chasing up and if you do become that person, your business relationships would likely deteriorate because no one wants to do business with someone that doesn't want to or can't pay them for any reason.

Want to keep your business relationships on track? It's simple. Just monitor what bills you need to pay... and pay them. No excuses there!

Stock or Inventory Management

Let's go back to the refrigerator example in this section and imagine that you live with two housemates. One that is "extra" in their purchasing of groceries (they purchase two of everything) and your other housemate is one that doesn't really plan out what they need and just picks up a few items.

The "extra" housemate often has food in the refrigerator that has spoiled or is decaying. This is because they purchase way too much that they can't eat all of it, and then it goes to waste. On the other hand, the other housemate often finds that they don't have enough to eat because they didn't buy enough.

On the one hand, you have wastage, not just from food but of the money that was used to purchase the food that is now decaying. On the other hand, you have not enough food and the resulting housemate being hungry.

Both aren't ideal situations. And it's these unideal situations that also make their way into inventory. When a business purchases too much stock, they risk lack of demand if the item has gone out of fashion, but there's also the cost of storing the items. Quite simply, there is wastage. When a business doesn't buy enough inventory, it may struggle to meet demand if there is a surge or an uptick in interest. In such a case, the business "misses out" on the sales that could have been. In both, financial losses are possible.

So how best to deal with this?

In the case of your housemates, the "extra" one could write down what's spoiling and not purchase that item. This would reduce the items they're purchasing. For your hungry housemate, they could note down what's missing and that could form a shopping list for the week.

But the key is having information.

If you manage your inventory in your accounting system separately, there's a high chance that there are multiple types of inventory management reports available for you which can help you look at the profit margin of your items (whether you're making money on what you're selling) and also the quantity of inventory you have on hand.

Good practice would be to decide on a regular review schedule for your inventory reports. It could be weekly, monthly or whatever period that works with your business needs. You'd review how many items you have on hand (and check that you do indeed have that same amount in physical stock—theft and loss can happen), how they're selling and then make decisions as to how to optimally manage your inventory.

There can be a range of ways, such as:

‣ Making a rule to purchase an item when the stock levels hit a certain amount. This might help to keep your item in stock to meet any sales.

‣ Organizing a stocktake "sale" promotion to get rid of excess inventory through a quick sale and to make room for new inventory.

- Choosing to order stock only when there is a sale so that it is housed in your warehouse for only a short period of time before dispatch.

- Not buying in bulk, unless there is a high chance that you can sell the items.

Managing your inventory, if you have inventory, is part of running a healthy business.

To do that, you need to first have your records (which you do!) and then review the reports and make decisions. Decisions that reduce wastage and meet sales as they come. Because decaying food and being hungry aren't two options you really want!

Filings and Lodgments

One of the major tasks you may likely have to do as a business owner is lodge statements or returns to the authorities.

This is one of the harder things to do because you really have to make sure:

- The information you're relying on, i.e. your records, are as correct and complete as possible.

- Calculations are performed correctly so that you're not underpaying or overpaying.

- You fill in the forms correctly and use the correct forms (if you have forms). That's sometimes the hardest part, right? Understanding what some of the words on the forms mean given the multiple aliases that finance words tend to have!

- You complete your forms and any associated payments on time.

The thing is that you might have many reporting requirements due at different time frames to different authorities so the first thing you should do is: determine what you need to report, to whom, how and by when.

I like to set mine up in a table like this:

Report	Who	How	When
Income tax	Tax office	Via accountant	End of year
Monthly sales tax	Comptroller	Via accountant	On 28th of the following month

And then, because I don't want to miss a deadline, I'll set up two automatic calendar reminders. One that's a few weeks out, so that the work can be started and then one a week or so before the deadline so that lodgment or filing can be done on time.

But, then again, I'm the type of person that menu plans two weeks in advance, just because.

As each business differs in its requirements, it's important to consult a qualified professional that can help you ascertain and set up what reporting you need to do and when.

It's something you really need to just establish at the beginning and then review periodically if your requirements change or there are other obligations that have recently come about or if existing obligations change.

This is not really something that is negotiable.

If you don't meet your obligations to your authorities, you could be up for penalties and/or interest. And that would be just the start of the pain and stress.

After learning how to manage your money by starting with the basics—record-keeping, you've transitioned to the higher level skills of reviewing reports and making decisions to help improve your business but also to help you meet obligations you might have to authority bodies.

You really have started out strong. Well done, boss!

Try it Yourself

Sometimes, it's nice to road-test things prior to doing it on your "real" records. Doing a road-test helps you pick up new practices and allows you to really orientate yourself around this whole process of record-keeping. For many of you, it's a new process and they'll be little things along the way that you might have to pick up and learn.

The following activities have been designed to allow you to use your own chosen accounting software. And when I complete these activities, I'll be using manager.io which is currently available as a free desktop download so some formatting may be different, but the substance of the results of our record-keeping should be the same.

In this section, you'll be able to practice record-keeping based on certain types of businesses. You'll receive some "proof documentation" and other details that you'll need to keep records. You'll also have a bank reconciliation that you'll need to complete.

These are all included in the next few sections of this book, but the electronic files (like a QIF bank reconciliation file) are also available for you via the members-only section on usefulmoneystuff.com if you'd like to simulate a typical workflow using electronic resources only.

Once you complete all your record-keeping, you'll go into your accounts section and see if the balance of each of your accounts (that's the end number after you've added and taken away things that have gone into a specific account) matches that of the results shown in the results section.

If there are any inconsistencies, we recommend you trace back your steps as problem-solving is also part of record-keeping. Sometimes, differences can also be due to simple mistakes made in record-keeping, like pressing 1 instead of 2. And yes, these mistakes also happen in real life, that's why checking your records is crucial!

Let's assume that in these example companies, they're trading as sole proprietors, they're doing cash accounting and they live in an area where there are no taxes applied at the point of making a sale! Lucky!

Ready to start?

Let's look at the example businesses now and let's try to help them start out strong with managing their money!

Social Media Influencer

Yes. Social media influencers are legit business people, no matter what other people think or say.

If you're a content creator or influencer, we see you and if others don't, that's just because you're ahead of your time. Influencers are in the business of content creation and marketing.

When you think about content, it used to be in the hands of big media companies. With social media, people can choose where they want their content from and follow these content creators and just like media companies could earn income from sponsored ads, selling their access to their content, advertising and other income-earning activities, so too can influencers.

Let's get ahead in your money management.

The details

This social media influencer posts a range of content and has 50,000 followers and 2,000 paid subscribers each paying $2.99

a month to exclusive access content. They're finding that they need to manage their money because it wasn't really organized at all, and things have picked up with their follower count.

For example, they're now selling custom video messages. They've also partnered this month with a teeth whitening company that wants them to do a sponsored post. And... this influencer is also running ads on a radio station to boost their follower count.

Let's do this!

Use your chosen accounting software to:

1. Set up suitable accounts that you'll use to 'store' your sales or purchase invoices. Remember the section earlier in the book called "Set Up Your Financial Refrigerator"? That section went through the account creation process and you're going to do that now for this business.

2. Set up one bank account.

3. Record the 'proof documentation' below using accounts available to you via your accounting system—whether automatically created by your system or whether you created them in Step 1.

4. Once done, do your bank reconciliation.

A bank statement has been provided in one of the sections below. If you use the bank statement provided in this book, you may need to individually enter each transaction line item in your bank account in your accounting software or import them according to how your accounting software works.

Once you have completed your recording and bank reconciliation, check the results section to see if everything matches. If so, you've done your record-keeping for the month! Well done!

If it doesn't match—and this happens in real-life situations too, check back to see what should be fixed in order to get a match.

The documents

Below are all the documents this business has on hand as part of their business activities for this month. Use these documents to record, where possible. There may be some missing details like email addresses etc... and where there are, you'll be able to use your own chosen dummy entries. Please do not use dummy figures or numbers. The purpose of this activity is so that the records are entered in appropriately where they matter.

It's important to make sure that you do your checks on the documents when you record them into your accounting system via your accounting software. Have the amounts been entered in correctly? Have you created invoices where supposed to and where none existed previously? Do your dates match? Do your totals match?

Subscriber Sales Compensation Report for this month. Paid on last day of the month.

Tier	Quantity	Net Compensation	Total
Basic	2000	2.50	$5000
Premium	0	5.50	0
Total compensation			**$5000**

Terms of subscription website...
....A fee of $0.49 is deducted by us from the price paid by the subscriber. You receive the remaining amount after this fee is applied....

Date: 5th day of this month.

Hey Beth,

Thanks so much for your order. I confirm that payment of $10 has been received and your custom video has now been created!
You'll be able to access it here: random_link
Thanks so much for ordering with us!

Bank terms...
....There is a service fee of $20 that is automatically deducted from your account at the end of the month....

Date: 3rd of this month. From: the big company.
We're a big company and we'd like you to do a sponsored post this month on the 15th day. We'll pay you $1000 for the post.

Date: 15th of this month. From: you.
Sure, the post it done now and my bank details for payment are: 111111111

Date: 16th of this month. From: the big company
We saw the post! It's amazing. Great job. Sure, we'll get accounts to make payment today. Should be in your account in 3-5 days time. Love your work and thanks again!

Invoice: 2309801
Date: 8th of this month

To: you

From: Radio station advertising department

Description:

1 x radio advertising over 2nd weekend of this month

Total: $3300
Pay to bank account 222222
Payment due: 11th day of this month.

The bank reconciliation

The bank statement for this month ("TM") has been provided
for you below. Use this bank statement to perform your bank
reconciliation. Each software does do its bank reconciliation in
its own individual way. With the software I'm using, I enter in
all the sales and purchases and then I receipt them as cleared
received or put them down as cleared payments—only if I see
them in the bank statement. Then I put the balance in my bank
account and if it matches, the reconciliation is largely done.

Don't forget, it's important to do your checks.

What checks? Well... make sure that you've transposed the correct amounts, that debit amounts aren't accidentally entered as credits and vice versa, that your opening balance was entered correctly and that finally, your closing balance matches the balance shown in your bank in your accounting software.

Your bank reconciliation may bring up some discrepancies and you'll be able to check if you've picked up on these discrepancies in the next section, "The results".

Date	Description	Debit	Credit	Balance
TM, 1	Opening balance			4,029
TM, 4	Beth – vid		10	4,039
TM, 10	Advertising	3000		1,039
TM, 10	Advertising	300		739
TM, 31	Content Subs Service		5000	5,739
TM, 31	Bank service fees	20		5,719
Balance on final date of TM				**5,719**

The results

After you've done your bank reconciliation, did you pick up the following inconsistencies requiring further follow up?

‣ Payment from "The Big Company" was never received. An invoice should have been created to detect that this amount was owing to you and a follow up communication requesting payment immediately should be done without delay.

Your accounts (usually this report is called a "Trial Balance") should show the following balances for this month and assume all accounts had a zero balance prior, except where a previous balance was provided:

▸ Sales: $6,990. This is made up of $10 from Beth, $5980 from subscribers and $1,000 from Big Company. You'll note that even if you choose "cash accounting" these sales will appear in the account. It's when it comes to "reporting" time that your accounting software should only report sales that were received in cash—so that means it would exclude the $1,000 from Big Company. You'll also see that it's $5,980 not $5000 from the content subscription site—the money earned from your subscribers was higher, but then the fees of $980 were applied in a separate account. Finally, I've chosen to put all sales together under the "Sales" category but remember, it's your business, so if you feel that setting it up in three different categories like "Subscription Sales", "Video sales" and "Advertising sales" gives you more relevant information, then more power to you!

▸ Advertising and promotion: $3,300

▸ Bank charges: $20

- Subscription site fees: $980. This was an account I created to take into consideration accounting for these costs.

- Accounts receivable: $1,000. This is the amount that you're supposed to receive from... The Big Company.

- Cash at bank: $5719. This is the amount in your bank account at a certain date.

All good and matched up? Great. Proceed to the next business.

Nope? Then go back and work through your numbers to see where there are differences. Take it from experience, this won't be the first time you'll be doing it. It's not unusual in accounting to look back and find mistakes.

Gig Workers / Independent Contractors / Consultants

When you're a consultant, independent contractor or gig worker —your time is your money.

This group encompasses a range of industries—you could be a ride-share driver, an artist, a musician, a health consultant, a personal trainer, a babysitter, a hairdresser, a dog walker, a tutor, a stylist, a make-up artist, a writer, a web-developer, a photographer, a designer ... and the list goes on.

You might need equipment to perform your role, you might even have room hire and overhead costs for the use of administration or other services, but your core business is what you deliver with your time.

More and more people are independently contracting, whether that's full-time or as side gigs to help earn a bit of income. But what happens when you suspect that your side (or main) gig isn't earning income, but that it's costing you to maintain it? Or whether your dream to deliver 50 shows ends up resulting in a measly $1.40 an hour after you pay everything else? Or whether you're spending time on a client performing 'free services' that really make it not worth your time?

It's time to have the finances in order so that this information is available for you to review and make business decisions.

Whether it's your full-time role or a side-gig, go forth and start out strong with managing your money.

The details

This motivational, life and fitness coach (talk about a triple threat) delivers online video one-on-one consultations to their clients. They also spend the first three Sundays of the month driving as a ride-share driver. They're not sure if they're even making any money as a ride-share driver given the cost of gas has gone up and they need to get a hold on their money management after being spooked as their friend received a letter from their tax authority.

Let's do this!

Use your chosen accounting software to:

1. Set up suitable accounts that you'll use to 'store' your sales or purchase invoices. Remember the section earlier in the book called "Set Up Your Financial Refrigerator"? That section went through the account creation process and you're going to do that now for this business.

2. Set up one bank account.

3. Record the 'proof documentation' below using accounts available to you via your accounting system—whether

automatically created by your system or whether you created them in Step 1.

4. Once done, do your bank reconciliation.

A bank statement has been provided in one of the sections below. If you use the bank statement provided in this book, you may need to individually enter each transaction line item in your bank account in your accounting software or import them according to how your accounting software works.

Once you have completed your recording and bank reconciliation, check the results section to see if everything matches. If so, you've done your record-keeping for the month! Well done!

If it doesn't match—and this also happens in real life situations too, check back to see what should be fixed in order to get a match.

The documents

This business person accepts bookings via a booking app and their ride-sharing is done via an app too. Those app providers then make a payout to this person after applying their fees. This person also fills up their gas tank on the Sunday that they do their ride-share driving and it is used completely by the end of their shift. The receipts for filling up their tank have also been provided.

Booking app compensation report

* Fee is for payment processing and is non-refundable

Description	Date	Amount	Amount Refunded	Fee*	Payout
Life C – Jacob	TM, 2	100		2.6	97.4
Fitness C – Max	TM, 7	150	150	3.9	-3.9
Life C – Emma	TM, 14	100		2.6	97.4
Fitness C – Max	TM, 20	150		3.9	146.1
Fitness C – Max	TM, 27	150		3.9	146.1
Fitness C – Kellie	TM, 28	70		1.82	68.18

Ride-share app compensation report

* Fee is non-refundable

Date	Description	Earnings, including tips	Fee*	Payout
1st Sunday of TM	7 trips	100	30	70
2nd Sunday of TM	4 trips	90	27	63
3rd Sunday of TM	3 trips	50	15	35

Receipt: 436902
Date: 1st Sunday of This Month

Gas Pump 3: $2.15 per gallon X 12 gallons

Total paid: $25.80
Payment method: card

Receipt: 459561
Date: 3rd Sunday of This Month

Gas Pump 2: $2.81 per gallon X 12 gallons

Total paid: $33.72
Payment method: card

Receipt: 465491
Date: 3rd Sunday of This Month

Gas Pump 3: $2.95 per gallon X 12 gallons

Total paid: $35.4
Payment method: card

The bank reconciliation

The bank statement for this month ("TM") has been provided for you below. Use this bank statement to perform your bank reconciliation. The details for this business are similar to the previous business, that is: each software is different, do your checks and try to pick up on discrepancies, if any exist.

Date	Description	Debit	Credit	Balance
TM, 1	Opening balance			322
TM, 8	Gasoline	25.80		
TM, 15	Gasoline	33.72		
TM, 22	Gasoline	35.40		
TM, 31	Ride-share app		168	
TM, 31	Booking app		551.28	
TM, 31	Bank service fees	20		
Balance on final date of TM				**926.36**

The results

In this instance, after doing your bank reconciliation, your amounts should match up. There aren't any discrepancies detected from the bank reconciliation, but it doesn't mean that it is error-free. In a real-life situation, there could be items missing from your documents or from your bank account that could mean incomplete records but that the discrepancy isn't yet detected. Ahhh, the complicated world of financial record-keeping.

Your accounts (usually this report is called a "Trial Balance") should show the following balances for this month and assume all accounts had a zero balance prior, except where a previous balance was provided:

▸ Sales: $960. This is the total sales amount from your ride-share app and booking-app. The amount fees are not deducted from this amount and it is shown as a 'gross' amount. That is, how much your customers from these apps paid for your services before any fees and refunds are applied. The fees and refunds are contained in their own account because I want to understand how much money I pay in fees and how much money is refunded. It's good to monitor this because if you find that you're issuing a lot of refunds, that might be something you want to look into and find the reason why it's happening. It could be your refund policy, it could be poor description, it could be poor product or service or it could be any other reason. But the point is that, keeping it in a separate account allows you to track it clearly. Keeping it bunched up under "Sales" makes things a bit harder to separate out. You can see the two accounts below now.

▸ Sales refunds: $150

▸ App fees: $90.72

▸ Bank charges: $20

▸ Motor vehicle expenses: $94.92

▸ Cash at bank: $926.36. This is the amount in your bank account at a certain date.

All good and matched up? Great. Proceed to the next business.

Nope? Then go back and work through your numbers to see where there are differences. Take it from experience, this won't be the first time you'll be doing it. It's not unusual in accounting to look back and find mistakes.

Products Business

One of the most common businesses that people start is a products business. If you go onto an online marketplace, you'll see the range of things that people can sell from clothes, books, toys, electronics, equipment, pet accessories, homewares... you name it and you'll likely find it on an online marketplace.

But a products business isn't just limited to physical products that you can hold in your hand. There are also digital products like software downloads, access to online courses, ebooks, digital downloads of patterns for hobbies and more.

And, you've also got perishable products or those that need to be delivered or collected under certain conditions to ensure they stay as they are. We're talking about plants, food—such as fresh fruits and vegetables, hot dogs and ice-cream!

Sometimes, products aren't always sold as stand-alone items and many existing businesses include products alongside other businesses like independent contracting. For example, a wedding celebrant might also sell floral arrangements to couples—in such a case, the celebrant delivers the service of officiating the marriage while the product is the floral arrangement that complements the main business.

And one that is commonly seen is when you go to the hairdresser and get a haircut. You might see shampoo, conditioners and other hair styling products that are available to purchase at your hairdresser.

Additionally, products are an interesting business in that they can be manufactured and created in-house, such as the person making homemade soaps or sauces or purchased from a supplier e.g. the ice-cream vendor that purchases pre-made ice-cream tubs to then scoop and sell as "ice-cream on a cone".

A products business is a very versatile business that many people start with but can grow into a huge business.

So let's start out strong with our product business' finances.

The details

A street-market enthusiast loves finding various vintage items when they go to their weekly street-market. Unfortunately, they now no longer have any room at their house to store anymore of these market treasures. So, they have decided to sell anything purchased in this month's haul at the market through an online marketplace. Just because there's no room to store it and to make some extra cash!

Let's do this!

Use your chosen accounting software to:

1. Set up suitable accounts that you'll use to 'store' your sales or purchase invoices. Remember the section earlier in the book called "Set Up Your Financial Refrigerator"? That section went through the account creation process and you're going to do that now for this business.

2. Set up one bank account.

3. Record the 'proof documentation' below using accounts available to you via your accounting system—whether automatically created by your system or whether you created them in Step 1.

4. Once done, do your bank reconciliation.

A bank statement has been provided in one of the sections below. If you use the bank statement provided in this book, you may need to individually enter each transaction line item in your bank account in your accounting software or import them according to how your accounting software works.

Once you have completed your recording and bank reconciliation, check the results section to see if everything matches. If so, you've done your record keeping for the month! Well done!

If it doesn't match—and this also happens in real life situations too, check back to see what should be fixed in order to get a match.

The documents

Below are the documents from the market stall this person visited this month and the payout summary from their online marketplace. They only visited once this month because they had other commitments. This business person wants to use the inventory module in their accounting software. If you have an inventory module, see if you can try using it!

Receipt: 47
Date: TM, 7

Market stall 34

2 x vintage earrings (each $15)..... $30
5 x rings (each $5)........................... $25
10 x scarves (each $1).....................$10

Total paid: $65
Payment method: card

Online marketplace compensation report

* Fee is non-refundable

Date	Description	Sale	Fee*	Payout
TM, 20	1 ring	32	3.2	28.8
TM, 21	1 scarf	19	1.90	17.10

Receipt: 498036
Date: TM, 25

Postal Service

Shipment 1................ $9.45
Shipment 2................ $9.45

Total paid: $18.90
Payment method: card

Bank terms...
....There is a service fee of $20 that is automatically deducted
from your account at the end of the month....
....If your account has insufficient funds, you will be charged an
overdraft fee of $10....

The bank reconciliation

The bank statement for this month ("TM") has been provided for you below. Use this bank statement to perform your bank reconciliation. The details for this business are similar to the previous business, that is: each software is different, do your checks and try to pick up on discrepancies, if any exist.

Date	Description	Debit	Credit	Balance
TM, 1	Opening balance			100
TM, 7	Market stall	95		5
TM, 25	Postal service	18.90		-13.9
TM, 31	Online marketplace		45.9	32
TM, 31	Overdraft fee	10		22
TM, 31	Bank service fees	20		2
Balance on final date of TM				**2**

The results

After you've done your bank reconciliation did you pick up the following inconsistencies requiring further follow up?

▸ It seems as though you were overcharged at the market stall. The full amount was $65 but they entered in $95 on the payment processing device. You do remember giving them your card to swipe but were busy looking at something else that you didn't see the amount being charged. You've got your two proof documents—your receipt from them and your bank statement, so you'll use those two things to get in touch with the market stall holder (you'll be going back this weekend for sure) to request a refund of the amount overcharged. Unfortunately, it looks like the overcharge of $30 led to your bank account having insufficient funds at one point in time and so your bank has also charged an overdraft fee! Always check you're being charged the right amount!! Note to self: do not become distracted when paying for something.

Your accounts (usually this report is called a "Trial Balance") should show the following balances for this month and assume all accounts had a zero balance prior, except where a previous balance was provided:

▸ Inventory - sales: $51. If you've used your inventory module, usually the system sets you up with an automatic inventory sales account to track sales of inventory. Remember, the fees are accounted for separately (so in an invoice, I put inventory and beneath it, a line that goes to the online marketplace fees account (which I created under 'expenses') for a -$5.10. The negative number in the sales invoice means that it will reduce the amount of the total in the end. This $5.10 is stored in a separate account—see below.

▸ Online marketplace fees: $5.10

- Postage: $18.90

- Bank charges: $30. This was higher by $10 due to not having sufficient funds as a result of the market stall holder overcharging.

- Inventory cost (under expenses): $6.00. If you're using the inventory module, this section means that the two inventory items you've bought previously and held, have now been sold and the cost of selling them was $6.00 (this is how much you bought them for).

- Inventory on hand: $59. This is the amount of the haul of your market day that's remaining. This is the inventory that's still on hand and wasn't sold. This means you have $59 worth of market haul finds that you weren't able to sell this month.

- Cash at bank: $32 or $2 depending on how you did your bank reconciliation. The difference is the $30 that needs to be resolved. Either refunded back to you, you increase the cost of your inventory or something else. The sensible decision to make is yours.

In the last three activities, you've done (and good on you), you had the ease of not having to worry about how taxation may impact your invoices—both sales and purchases.

In real life, you most likely have to deal with taxation. But...see it as a component of your record-keeping.

For this area, it is important that you consult with a qualified professional in your area who can provide you with taxation advice on how you should be dealing with taxation when it comes to your sales and purchases. There might be certain tax rates that apply in certain instances. Your taxation professional would likely be the person who is in the best position to help you.

After all of this, now check your results for the final business. If your results don't match up, go back to your records and find out why. It could be a typo or any other mistake. Whatever it is, find it and fix it up.

Are we all good and matched up?

Nice work! You've reached the end... of an ongoing cycle.

A Profitable Business

Now that you're in a cycle of record-keeping and using those records to do basic money management moves in your business, it's time to turn back to the primary goal of your business—and that's making a profit.

How does a business make a profit and how can you see that your business is making one?

The easiest way to understand this would be at an intuitive and basic level, so let's assume that you are a stocking associate or stocking clerk. You get paid $705 a week with tax already taken out. In your normal activities during the week, you might watch tv, live in a share house, shower and care for yourself, eat food, use electricity, use water, drive to work and do some sports. Let's say all these activities cost you $455 a week. Based on the activities that bring in money (work) and the activities that spend money (practically living), you've got $250 left over.

Intuitively, what this means is that the activities that you're doing are creating a reserve of money left over that you can access to do what you want. And that's profit.

It's when a business, during a set period of time that's considered, has activities that have brought in more money than the activities that they've spent.

It might be that in some months or weeks, a business makes a loss (spends more than the money they make) and sometimes this is legitimate, if they're going through an expansion. But, on the whole, you want to see a business having that 'spare' amount overall over time because that's profit and that's the goal in a business.

Now we get to the next part of the question.

How can you see that your business is making one?

Well... you know your record-keeping, the one that's used for reports to chase up on delinquent payments (fun times right?), pay people on time and provide you with financial information that you may need to report to the authorities, well... there's another use for it too...

Super intel and insight, of the business kind.

There is a specific report called a "Profit and Loss" report, or it could also be known by its other names like "Income Statement", that is generally available in most accounting software in the "Reports" section.

This is the report that uses the information you record to let you know how all your business activities lead in terms of financial performance. Are the activities leading to a profit considering the whole year, are you breaking-even (where you don't make a profit or a loss) or have you made a loss?

The number you want to look at first to get this answer is usually the bottom one which has the overall profit/loss figure.

The next step is to figure out how to improve the bottom figure and it starts with looking at that report (can you see how important it is now to get your recording correct and complete as possible?).

We see the bigger number, but the lines that make up the bigger number are where you'll be able to find areas where you can improve your profit or loss figure.

Sometimes it might be deciding to cut out travel costs altogether and switching to virtual communications. It might be switching to a different courier provider. It might also require leveraging from the "players" in your game to help fund new lines or to review certain conditions.

Whatever it is in your business, it will most likely be found within the information shown in your reports, from the records that you keep.

Making a business profitable comes through ongoing action and tweaking of your business to deal with the changes in your environment. And just like a person, a business grows and changes through time. Things that worked before, may not work in two weeks' time.

Your record-keeping might evolve to where you'll have add-ons to deal with changes—say for example, you hire new employees because the business can afford employees now. You might have to add on a payroll module in your accounting software (not covered in this book because it is outside the scope) to be able to record your payments to employees and their entitlements.

But what should be there as your business evolves, is the record-keeping (even if you expand it). It's there to witness and record all the goings-on, just like a diary, but better.

This is the information that you'll need to make those business decisions and it's this financial information that is, ultimately, invaluable to the running of your business.

So, go forth and conquer, and make decisions to enhance your business, because after all, you're starting out strong.

Let's Keep in Touch, *Really*!

Let's face it, starting a business is hard. And people don't realize how hard it is until they have to open their accounting software and start recording money stuff!

We'd love to hear about your stories and can be contacted at:

www.usefulmoneystuff.com (Psst. you can also use this site to find an accountant for help!)

Instagram: **useful_money_stuff**

Youtube: **https://www.youtube.com/usefulmoneystuff**

Make Money Moves:

How to Read & Understand Financial Reports, the *Easy* Way

New book coming out soon!
Pre-order now at usefulmoneystuff.com

Understanding your business's finances is a serious super-power.

Imagine being able to make confident decisions like cutting out a product line or setting up a shopfront because you've got the intel that the particular product line isn't making any money or that your sales are booming in a particular geographical area. Or even being able to make investment decisions on a company... Backed. By. Data.

Good business decisions are based on reliable information which is actually found around quite a bit—financial statements anyone?

The problem is being able to make sense of the financial statements (we're talking income statement/profit and loss, statement of financial position/balance sheet and cash flow) so that you too can start making data-backed decisions.

That's where this book completes your missing link—using intuitive examples that relate to real life and written in simple English, with this book, you'll learn how to read and understand financial reports, the easy way.

And, most importantly, you'll unlock this super-power and be making serious money moves.

www.ingramcontent.com/pod-product-compliance
Lightning Source LLC
Chambersburg PA
CBHW011842200326
41597CB00026B/4677